FORGIVENESS

Also by Osho

INSIGHTS FOR A NEW WAY OF LIVING

Awareness

Compassion

Courage

Creativity

Forgiveness

Freedom

Happiness

Intelligence

Intimacy

Intuition

Joy

Maturity

Trust

FORGIVENESS

The Strength
Lies in Anger

OSHO

•

INSIGHTS FOR A
NEW WAY OF LIVING

ST. MARTIN'S
ESSENTIALS
NEW YORK

Published in the United States by St. Martin's Essentials,
an imprint of St. Martin's Publishing Group

The material in this book is selected from various talks by Osho given to a live
audience. All of Osho's talks have been published in full as books and are also available
as original audio recordings. Audio recordings and the complete text archive can be
found via the online OSHO Library at www.osho.com.

OSHO® is a registered trademark of OSHO International Foundation,
www.osho.com/trademarks.

www.stmartins.com

The Library of Congress Cataloging-in-Publication Data is available upon request.

ISBN 978-1-250-78634-0 (trade paperback)
ISBN 978-1-250-78635-7 (ebook)

Our books may be purchased in bulk for promotional, educational, or business use.
Please contact your local bookseller or the Macmillan Corporate and
Premium Sales Department at 1-800-221-7945, extension 5442, or
by email at MacmillanSpecialMarkets@macmillan.com.

First St. Martin's Essentials Edition: 2023

10 9 8 7 6 5 4 3 2 1

Contents

Contents

Introduction

When the word or subject of forgiveness comes up in Osho's talks, it is generally as a byproduct—of becoming aware, of "taking space," of realizing that nursing hurt feelings or fantasies of revenge harms no one more than oneself. Forgiveness, unlike many of the other titles in the *Insights for a New Way of Living* series, is not a word that Osho often uses. At its simplest level—where the word is not a concern at all—forgiveness is what happens when we let go of (or, sometimes, work through) all that is non-existential and meaningless in the here and now of our lives.

This is where a related word, *repentance*, comes in. Say we were "triggered" by something and reacted: we got angry. We lashed out at another with the intent to hurt them, we said things we wish we hadn't said. It is an opportunity to remember that our task—our first task—is to take note of it, to own it, to acknowledge it, to take responsibility for it. And, if we find that indeed we acted unconsciously and wrongly, to *repent*—meaningfully, with full awareness—so that it doesn't happen again.

As we learn in these pages, on another level "forgiveness" is a uniquely religious approach to a shared problem of our human-ness—animals don't suffer from this problem—which is our tendency to do things that we later wish we hadn't done. Or, for that matter, to do things that we *want* to do, despite the fact that our parents, our churches, our teachers have told us they are "sinful" or "wrong." So we need forgiveness because we have done these things anyway. In the Judeo-Christian context, we spend a lot of time praying to be delivered from evil, led not into temptation, then forgiven when we go astray. Forgiveness is a prerequisite to become happy or redeemed.

In the East, on the other hand, the idea of "karma" takes care of most of that stuff. The hell we are living in now is a natural consequence of our bad acts in the past. The happiness we experience now, the riches or the good reputation, are our reward for having behaved well in the past. And furthermore, where Christianity gives us only one life to sort all this out, the Eastern religions give us many lives. "Forgiveness" is a minor, bit player in the karmic drama we're all engaged in here. We can take our time; there is no "judgment day" on the horizon where we'll have to slip in under the wire or be lost forever.

In this book, Osho unpacks all the nuances, examines all the roots, and sheds light on the intersections where Eastern and

Western approaches to the concept of forgiveness—and its related concepts of sin and guilt, shame and repentance, and their past, present, and future consequences—meet.

—Sarito Carol Neiman, compiler and editor

Osho International Foundation

A Note About Language

Spoken Words: Osho's books are not "written," but rather are transcribed from recordings of his talks. These talks are extemporaneous, without reference to notes other than copies of questions, stories, or scriptures he has been asked to comment upon, or jokes he might use to drive home a particular point. He has asked his editors to preserve that quality of the spoken word in his printed books.

Pronouns: When hearing him speak, it is quite clear to the listener that generally when Osho talks about "man," he is referring to "human beings." His use of "he" as a default pronoun simply serves an ease and flow of speaking—in no way does it imply that "she" (or "they") is being dismissed or disregarded.

Osho's unique vantage point is good to keep in mind:

A meditator is neither a man nor a woman,
because meditation has nothing to do with your body;
neither does it have anything to do with your mind.
In meditation you are simply and purely consciousness.
And consciousness is neither male nor female.

FORGIVENESS

1

Forgiveness:
The Ideal Versus the Actual

We have been talking about love for thousands of years, but where is love in our life? We have been talking about forgiveness and serving humanity, but where is forgiveness, and where is service to humanity? And our service to humanity and our forgiveness have become servants to our deepest vested interest. Someone wants to attain to liberation or to go to heaven—that is why he forgives and he gives to charity. But is it really forgiveness and charity, or is it a bargain? Someone wants to find his soul, so he serves the poor. But is it really serving the poor, or is it just making a poor person an instrument for one's own vested interest?

All this social service, all this charity, all this forgiveness, and all this nonsense of nonviolence hides the real person who is there inside us. And that real person who is there—only that person exists. If anything has to happen at all, then it has to happen through that person. Any sort of revolution in life, any sort of change in life—anything that needs to happen—has to happen through that real human being. It has to happen through that actual person that I am, that you are. Nothing is going to happen through any ideals.

But we hide ourselves in ideals. A bad man, in trying to become good, can forget that he is a bad man—he wants to forget that he is a bad person. This is the way all such people cling to good ideals.

> It has to happen through that actual person that I am, that you are. Nothing is going to happen through any ideals.

If someone talks about high ideals, then know that a bad person is present inside him. If a bad person is not present inside, then he simply cannot talk about "high ideals"—because then the person himself will be good! Then what is there to talk about? Where does the question of high ideals arise?

A "high ideal" is a trick of the bad person who is hidden inside us, and it is a very subtle trick by which we defend ourselves. In trying to become good, we forget the bad. But as long as the bad is present inside, can anyone become good? We may try in a thousand and one ways, but whatever we do, the bad person will again come back from inside.

This is the reality all around us—but perhaps you have lost the ability to see it. The bad person is present inside you, the one who is full of violence and hatred. Whatever you may do, howsoever virtuous an act you may do, since that bad person is present behind your virtuous act, it is going to be a deception. Behind that act, the reality is something else. It is possible that it may not be visible from outside; perhaps it may not be visible to others, but you have the ability to see it.

And if you can see it, then you can start on the journey of acquiring a healthy mind; you can travel the path toward a healthy being. So the first thing is to take the first step on the journey, the first step in the direction of acquiring a healthy mind, a healthy consciousness.

> No one has ever been transformed by an ideal. From outside, it may appear that someone has changed, but the same person will be present inside.

The first thing is to see the truth of yourself *as a fact*, and not as your ideal is. What is your actuality? Not what is your ideology, not what do you believe, but what are you? What is your reality?

If you can be ready to know that—and only then—you can drop this meaningless idea from your mind: the idea that you can change, that you can become transformed by having ideals and being in competition to have the highest ideals. No one has ever been transformed by an ideal. From outside, it may appear that someone has changed, but the same person will be present inside.

The Strength of Forgiveness Lies in Anger

The whole of mankind has become schizophrenic. Man's mind is split into parts, into fragments, and there is a reason for this: we have taken the totality of life as if it were made up of parts, and we have pitted each part against the other.

Man is one, but we have created divisions inside, and have also determined that these divisions are contrary to each other. We have done this in all spheres. We tell a person, "Don't be angry, be forgiving"—without realizing that the difference between anger and forgiveness is again only of degrees.

As it is between cold and hot, between childhood and old age, we can say that anger, reduced to the lowest degree, is forgiveness—there is no dichotomy between them. But all the age-old precepts of mankind teach us: "Get rid of anger and adopt forgiveness." As if anger and forgiveness are such opposite things that you can drop anger and retain forgiveness. Such a thing can only result in splitting people into fragments and in bringing them trouble.

In life, everything is integrated. It is like the notes of a great symphony. If you cut anything out, you will find yourself in difficulty. Someone may say the color black signifies evil. That's why no one is allowed to wear black at marriages; black is allowed at somebody's death. There are people who believe black is a sign of evil, and there are people who believe white is a sign of purity.

In a symbolic sense, it is alright to have such distinctions, but if someone were to say, "Let's get rid of black; let's remove black from the face of the earth," then remember: with the removal of black, very little white will be left behind, because the whiteness of white stands out in all its sharpness only against a black background.

The teacher writes on a blackboard with white chalk. Is he out of his mind? Why doesn't he write on the white wall? Of course one can write on a white wall, but the letters won't stand out. White manifests because of the black background; black is, in fact, causing the white to stand out. And remember, someone who becomes inimical to any one side of a duality causes the other side to become dull and faded as well.

One who is against showing anger, his forgiveness will be impotent. The strength of forgiveness lies in anger; only one who can be angry has the power to be forgiving. The more fierce the anger, that much greater will be the forgiveness. The power of anger itself will lend luster to the act of forgiveness. In the absence of anger, the forgiveness will appear totally lackluster, absolutely lifeless, dead.

> Only one who can be angry has the power to be forgiving. The more fierce the anger, that much greater will be the forgiveness.

Apology Is Needed Because There Is No Relationship

If a man steps on a stranger's foot in the marketplace, he
  makes a polite apology and offers an explanation: "This
  place is so crowded."
If an elder brother steps on his younger brother's foot, he says,
  "Sorry," and that is that.
If a parent treads on his child's foot, nothing is said at all.
The greatest politeness is free of all formality. Perfect conduct
  is free of concern.
Perfect wisdom is unplanned. Perfect love is without demon-
  strations. Perfect sincerity offers no guarantee.

—*Chuang Tʒu*

Apology is needed because there is no relationship. The other is a stranger: explanation is needed because there is no love.

If there is love, then there is no need for an explanation: the other will understand. If there is love, there is no need for apology: the other will understand. Love always understands, so there is no higher morality than love—there cannot be.

Love is the highest law—but if it is not there, then substitutes are needed. Stepping on a stranger's foot in the marketplace, an apology is needed—and an explanation, also: "This place is so crowded."

In reference to this, one thing has to be understood: in the West, even a husband will offer an apology; a wife will offer an explanation. It means that love has disappeared; it means that everybody has become a stranger, that there is no home—that every place has become a marketplace.

In the East, it is impossible to conceive of this state—but Westerners think that Easterners are rude. A husband will never give an explanation—no need, because we are not strangers, and the other can understand. When the other cannot understand, only then is an apology needed. And if love cannot understand, what good is an apology going to do?

If the world becomes a home, all apologies will disappear, all explanations will disappear. You give explanations because you are not certain about the other. Explanation is a trick to avoid conflict; apology is a device to avoid conflict.

But the conflict is there, and you are afraid of it—this is a civilized way to get out of the conflict. You have stepped on a stranger's foot. You look—violence is in his eyes; he has become aggressive; he will hit you. Apology is needed, and his anger will subside with an apology. It is a trick—you need not be authentic in your apology; it is just a social device. It works as a lubricant. Then you give an explanation, just to say, "I am not responsible; the place is so crowded. It is a marketplace; nothing can be done; it had to happen." The explanation says that you are not responsible.

Love is always responsible, whether the place is crowded or not, because love is always aware and alert. You cannot shift the responsibility to the situation: you are responsible. Look at this

> Love is always responsible, whether the place is crowded or not, because love is always aware and alert. You cannot shift the responsibility to the situation: you are responsible.

phenomenon—apology is a device, just like a lubricant, to avoid conflict. And explanation is shifting the responsibility onto something else. You don't say, "I was unconscious, unaware, that is why I stepped on your foot." You say, "The place is so crowded!" A conscious person cannot do this—and if you go on doing this, you will never become truly religious.

Because true religiousness means taking all the responsibility that is there—not avoiding, not escaping. The more responsible you are, the more awareness will arise out of it; the less you feel responsible, the more and more unconscious you will become. Whenever you feel that you are not responsible, you will go to sleep.

And this has happened—not only in individual relationships; on all levels of society this has happened. Marxism says that society is responsible for everything. If a person is poor, society is responsible; if a person is a thief, society is responsible. You are not responsible; no individual is responsible. Marxism shifts the whole responsibility onto society; you are not responsible.

Look at the religious attitude, which is totally different, qualitatively different. A religious person thinks himself responsible: If someone is begging, if a beggar is there, I am responsible. The beggar may be at the other end of the earth; I may not know him,

I may not come across his path, but if the beggar is there, I am responsible. If a war goes on anywhere—in Israel, in Vietnam, anywhere—I am not participating in it in any visible way, but I am responsible.

I am here. I cannot shift the responsibility onto society.

What do you mean when you say "society"? Where is this society? This is one of the greatest escapes. Only individuals exist; you will never come across society. You will never be able to pinpoint it: "This is society." Everywhere the individual is in existence, and society is just a word.

Where is society? Ancient civilizations played a trick. They said: God is responsible, fate is responsible. Now communism plays the same game, saying that society is responsible. But where is society? God may be somewhere; society is nowhere, there are only individuals. Religiousness says: I am responsible. No explanation is needed to avoid it.

And remember one thing more: whenever you feel that you are responsible for all the ugliness—for all the mess, anarchy, war, violence, aggression—suddenly you become alert. Responsibility penetrates your heart and makes you aware.

When you say, "This place is much too crowded," you can

> You will never be able to pinpoint it: "This is society." Everywhere the individual is in existence, and society is just a word.

go on walking sleepily. Really, you step on the stranger's foot not because the place is crowded but because you are unconscious. You are walking like a somnambulist, walking in your sleep. When you step on somebody's foot, you suddenly became aware because now there is danger. You make the apology, "The place is crowded!" Then you fall asleep and start moving again.

What are you really doing when you say "sorry"? Your sleep is broken, you were walking in a dream—you must have been dreaming, imagining, something was going on in the mind—and then you stepped on someone. Not that the place was crowded— you would have stumbled even if no one were there. If only a few people were there, even then you would have stepped on someone. It is you, your unconsciousness, your unconscious behavior. A Buddha cannot stumble even if it is a marketplace, because he moves with full consciousness. Whatsoever he is doing, he is doing it knowingly.

And if he steps on your foot, it means he has stepped knowingly; there must be some purpose in it. It may be just to help you wake up—just to make you awake, he may have stepped on your foot. But he will not say that "the place is crowded"; he will not give any explanation.

Explanations are always deceptive. They look logical, but they are false. You give explanations only when you have to hide something.

You can watch and observe this in your own life. This is not a theory, this is a simple fact of everybody's experience—you give explanations only when you want to hide something. Truth needs no explanation.

The more you lie, the more explanations are needed. There are so many scriptures because man has lied so much; then explanations are needed to hide the lies. You have to give an explanation, then this explanation will need further explanation, and it goes on and on. It is an

> You give explanations only when you have to hide something.

infinite regression. And even with the last explanation, nothing is explained. The basic lie remains a lie—you cannot convert a lie into a truth just by explaining it. You may think so, but nothing is explained by explanations.

Once it happened . . .

Mulla Nasruddin went on his first air trip, and he was afraid, but he didn't want anybody to know. It happens to everybody on their first air trip. Nobody wants everybody to know this is their first. He wanted to behave nonchalantly, so he walked very bravely. That bravery was an explanation: "I always travel by air." Then he sat down in his seat, and he wanted to say something just to make himself at ease, because whenever you start talking, you become brave; through talk, you feel less fear. So Nasruddin spoke to the passenger next to him.

He looked out of the window and said, "Look, what a height!
People look like ants."

The other man said, "Sir, we have not taken off yet.
Those are ants."

Explanations cannot hide anything. Rather, on the contrary, they reveal. If you can look, if you have eyes, every explanation is transparent. It would have been better if Nasruddin had been silent. But don't try silence as an explanation—as an explanation, it is of no use. Your silence will be revealing, and your words will reveal.

It is better not to be a liar; then you need not give any explanations. It is better to be truthful—the easiest thing is to be true and authentic. If you are afraid, it is better to say, "I am afraid," and, accepting the fact, your fear will disappear.

Acceptance is such a miracle. When you accept that you are afraid and say, "This is my first trip," suddenly you will feel a change coming over you.

The basic fear is not fear. The basic fear is the fear of the fear:

> The basic fear is not fear. The basic fear is the fear of the fear: "No one should know that I am afraid. No one should know that I am a coward."

"No one should know that I am afraid. No one should know that I am a coward." But everybody is a coward in a new situation—and in a new situation, to be brave will be foolish! To be cowardly only means that the situation is so new that your mind cannot supply any answers; the past cannot give the answers, so you are trembling. But this is good! Why try to supply an answer from the mind? Tremble, and let the answer come from your present consciousness. You are sensitive, that's all—don't kill this sensitivity through explanations.

Next time you start to give an explanation, be alert: What are you doing? Trying to hide something? Trying to explain away something? Nothing like this will be of any help.

Everywhere, Mirrors Are All Around You

A man who had become newly rich went to a beach, the most costly, expensive, the most exclusive, and he was spending madly just to influence the people around him. The next day, while swimming, his wife drowned. She was carried to the shore; a crowd gathered, so he asked, "What are you doing?"

One man said, "We are going to give your wife artificial respiration."

The rich man said, "Nothing doing; give her the real thing. I can pay for it."

Whatsoever you do, whatsoever you don't do—whatsoever you say, whatsoever you don't say—reveals you. Everywhere, mirrors are all around you. Every other person is a mirror; every situation is a mirror—whom do you think you are deceiving? And if it becomes a habit to deceive, ultimately you will have deceived yourself and no one else. It is your life that you are wasting in deceptions.

Chuang Tzu says: "Explanations show that you are not true, you are not authentic."

If an elder brother steps on his younger brother's foot, he says, "Sorry," and that is that.

Two brothers—when the relationship is more intimate, the other is not a stranger—then no explanation is needed. The brother simply says "sorry"; he accepts the blame. He says, "I have been unconscious." He is not shifting the responsibility onto somebody else: he accepts it, and that is that. The relationship is closer.

If a parent treads on his child's foot, nothing is said at all.

There is no need; the relationship is even closer, more intimate. There is love, and that love will do. No substitute is needed, no explanation, no apology.

The greatest politeness is free of all formality. Perfect conduct is free of concern.

Perfect wisdom is unplanned. Perfect love is without demonstrations. Perfect sincerity offers no guarantee.

But all these perfections need one thing, and that is spontaneous awareness; otherwise, you will always have false coins, you will always have false faces. You can be sincere—but if you have to make any effort, then that sincerity is just formal. You can be loving—but if your love needs effort, if your love is of the type that Dale Carnegie talks about in *How to Win Friends and Influence People*—if that type of love is there, it cannot be real. You have been manipulating it. Then even friendship is a business.

Beware of Dale Carnegies: these are dangerous people; they destroy all that is real and authentic. They show you how to "win friends"; they teach you tricks, techniques. They make you efficient; they give you the know-how. But love has no know-how; it cannot have. Love needs no training. And friendship is not something you have to learn—a learned friendship will not be a friendship, it will just be exploitation. You are exploiting the other and deceiving him; you are not true; this is a business relationship.

> Beware of Dale Carnegies: these are dangerous people; they destroy all that is real and authentic.

But in America, everything has become business—friendship and love also. And Dale Carnegie's books have sold millions of copies, hundreds of editions, next only to the Bible. Nobody knows how to be a friend; it has to be learned. Sooner or later there will be colleges for love, training courses, lessons you can learn and apply.

And the problem is that if you succeed, then you are lost forever, because the real will never happen to you; the door is completely closed. Once you become efficient in a certain thing, the mind resists change. The mind says this is the shortcut, and you know it well, so why choose another path? Mind is always for the least resistance.

That is why clever people are never able to love. They are so clever they start manipulating. They will not say what is in their heart, they will say what will appeal to the other. They will look at the other person and see what she wants to be said. They will not speak their heart; they will just create a situation in which the other is deceived. Husbands deceiving wives, wives deceiving husbands, friends deceiving friends . . .

The whole world has become just a crowd of enemies. There are only two types of enemies: those you have not been able to deceive and those you have been able to deceive. This is the only difference. Then how can there be ecstasy in your life?

So this is not a learning. Authenticity cannot come through schooling. Authenticity comes through awareness: if you are aware, if you live in a conscious way. Look at the difference: to live consciously means to live openly—not to hide, not to play games. To be alert means to be vulnerable, and whatsoever happens, happens. You accept it, but you never compromise; you never purchase anything by giving up your consciousness. Even if you are left totally alone, you will accept being left alone, but you will want to be consciously alert. Only in this alertness does real transformation start happening.

Only Alertness Can Help When the Whole World Is Mad

I will tell you a story:

It happened once, in ancient times: there was a king who was also an astrologer. He had a very deep interest in studying the stars. Suddenly there was panic in his heart because he became aware that the coming year's harvest was going to be dangerous. Whoever will eat the coming year's harvest will go mad.

So he called his prime minister, his adviser and counselor, and told him that this was going to happen, that it was a certainty. "The stars are clear: the combination of cosmic rays is such that this year's harvest is going to be poisonous. It happens rarely, in thousands of years, but this is going to happen this year, and anybody who will eat from that harvest will go mad. So . . . what should we do?"

The prime minister said, "It is impossible to provide for everybody from last year's harvest, but one thing can be done: you and I can both live on last year's harvest. Last year's harvest can be gathered, requisitioned. There is no problem; for you and me it will be enough."

The king said, "This doesn't appeal to me. Then all my devoted people will go mad: women, saints and sages, devoted servants, all my subjects, even children. And it doesn't appeal to me to be an outsider; it would not be worth saving just myself and you. That will not do; I would rather be mad with everybody else.

"But I have another suggestion," the king said. "I will mark your head with the seal of madness, and you will mark my head with the seal of madness."

"But," the prime minister said, "how is this going to help anybody?"

The king said, "I have heard it is one of the ancient pillars of wisdom, so let us try it. After everybody has gone mad—

after we have gone mad—whenever I look at your forehead, I will remember that I am mad. And whenever you look at my forehead, remember that you are mad."

The prime minister was still puzzled; he said, "But what will that do?"

The king said, "I have heard from wise men that if you can remember that you are mad, you are mad no longer."

A madman cannot remember that he is mad. An ignorant man cannot remember that he is ignorant. A man who is in a dream cannot remember that he is dreaming. If, in your dreams, you become alert and know that you are dreaming, the dream has stopped; you are fully awake. If you can understand that you are ignorant, ignorance drops.

Ignorant people go on believing that they are wise, and mad people think that they are the only really sane ones. When someone becomes really wise, he becomes so by recognizing his ignorance.

So the king said, "This we are going to do."

I don't know what happened; the story ends here, but the story is meaningful.

Only alertness can help when the whole world is mad, nothing else. Keeping yourself outside of it, going to the Himalayas, will not be of much help. When everyone is mad, you are going to be mad because you are

> When someone becomes really wise, he becomes so by recognizing his ignorance.

part and parcel of everybody; it is a totality, an organic totality. How can you separate yourself? How can you go to the Himalayas? Deep down, you remain part of the whole. Even living in the Himalayas you will remember your friends; they will knock in your dreams, you will think of them. You will wonder what they are thinking of you—you go on being related.

You cannot go out of the world. There is no place outside the world; the world is one continent. Nobody can be an island— even islands are joined with the continent deep down. You can just think superficially that you are separate, but nobody can be separate.

The king was really wise. He said, "It is not going to help. I am not going to be an outsider; I will be an insider, and this is what I will do. I will try to remember that I am mad, because when you forget that you are mad, then you are really mad. This is what is to be done."

Wherever you are, remember yourself: that you *are*. This consciousness that you are should become a continuity. Not your name, your caste, your nationality—those are futile things, absolutely useless. Just remember that "I am"; this must not be forgotten. This is what Hindus call self-remembrance, what Buddha called right mindfulness, what Gurdjieff used to call self-remembering, what Krishnamurti calls awareness. This is the most substantial part of meditation, to remember that "I am."

Walking, sitting, eating, talking, remember it: I am. Never forget this. It will be difficult, very arduous. In the beginning you will keep forgetting; there will be only single moments when you will feel illuminated, then it will be lost. But don't get miserable; even single moments are good. Go on, whenever you can remember—remember again, catch hold of the thread again. When you forget, don't worry—remember again, again catch hold of the thread, and by and by the gaps will lessen, the intervals will start dropping, a continuity will arise.

And whenever your consciousness becomes continuous, you need not use the mind. Then there is no planning, then you act out of your consciousness, not out of your mind. Then there is no need for any apology, no need to give any explanation. Then you are whatsoever you are; there is nothing to hide. Whatsoever you are, you are; you cannot do anything else. You can only be in a state of continuous remembrance. Through this remembrance, this mindfulness, comes the authentic religion, comes the authentic morality.

The Greatest Politeness Is Free of All Formality

If you are not formal, then nobody is a stranger. Whether you move in the marketplace or in a crowded street, nobody is a stranger; everybody is a friend. Not only a friend, really: everybody is just an extension of you. Then formality is not needed. If I step on my own foot—which is difficult—I will not say "sorry," and I will not say to myself, "The place is very crowded!"

When I step on your foot, I am stepping on my foot. A mind that is fully alert knows that consciousness is one, life is one, being is one, existence is one; it is not fragmented. The tree flowering there is me in a different form; the rock lying there on the ground is me in a different form. Then the whole of existence becomes an organic unity—organic, life flowing through it, not mechanical. A mechanical unity is a different thing—it is dead. A car is a mechanical unity; there is no life in it, and that is why you can replace one part with another. Every part is replaceable. But can you replace a human being? Impossible!

When a person dies, a unique phenomenon disappears—disappears completely, you cannot replace it. When your wife dies or your husband dies, now how can you replace them? You may get another wife, but this will be another wife, not a replacement. And the shadow of the first will always be there; the first cannot be forgotten, it will always be there. It may become a shadow, but even shadows of love are substantial.

Life is an organic unity. I say you cannot even replace a plant, because every plant is unique; you cannot find another, the same cannot be found. Life has a quality of uniqueness. Even a small rock is unique—you can go all over the world to find an identical rock and you will not be able to. How can you replace it? This is the difference between organic unity and mechanical unity. Mechanical unity depends on the parts; the

> Then your life becomes real, authentic, spontaneous. Then it is not formal; then you do not follow any rules.

parts are replaceable, they are not unique. Organic unity depends on the whole, not on the parts. Parts are not really parts, they are not separate from the whole—they are one, they cannot be replaced.

When you become alert to the inner flame of your inner being, suddenly you become alert that you are not an island; it is a vast continent, an infinite continent. There are no boundaries separating you from it. All boundaries are false, make-believe. All boundaries are in the mind; in existence there are no boundaries. Then who is a stranger? When you step on somebody, it is you; you have stepped on your own foot. No apology is needed, no explanation is needed. There is no one else, there is only one.

Then your life becomes real, authentic, spontaneous. Then it is not formal; then you do not follow any rules. You have come to know the ultimate law: now no rules are needed. You have become the law—there is no need to remember the rules now.

The greatest politeness is free of all formality.

It happened that Confucius came to see Lao Tzu, Chuang Tzu's master. And Confucius was the image of formal politeness. He was the greatest formalist in the world; the world has never known such a great formalist. He was simply manners, formality, culture, etiquette. He came to see Lao Tzu, the polar opposite.

Confucius was very old, and Lao Tzu was not so old. So to be formal when Confucius came in, Lao Tzu should have stood up to receive him. But he remained sitting. It was impossible for Confucius to believe that such a great master, known all over the country for his humbleness, should be so impolite! He had to talk about it.

Immediately he said, "This is not good. I am older than you."

Lao Tzu laughed loudly and said, "Nobody is older than me. I existed before everything came into existence. Confucius, we are of the same age, everything is of the same age. From eternity we have been in existence, so don't carry this burden of old age. Sit down."

Confucius had come to ask some questions. He said, "How should a religious man behave?"

Lao Tzu said, "When the how comes in, there is no religion. 'How' is not a question for a religious man. The how shows that you are not religious but that you want to behave like a religious man—that is why you ask how."

Does a lover ask how one should love? He loves! Really, it is only later on that he becomes aware that he has been in love. It may be that when the lover has gone he becomes aware that he has been in love. He simply loves. It happens. It is a happening, not a doing.

Whatsoever Confucius asked, Lao Tzu replied in such a way that Confucius became very disturbed: "This man is dangerous!" He went back; his disciples asked, "What happened, what manner of man is this Lao Tzu?"

Confucius said, "Don't go near him. You may have seen dangerous snakes, but nothing compares with this man. You may have heard about ferocious lions; they are nothing before this man. This man is a dragon walking on the earth; he can swim in the sea, he can go to the very end of the sky—very dangerous. He is not for us little people. We are too small. He is dangerous, vast like an abyss. Don't go near him; otherwise, you will feel dizzy and you may fall. Even I felt dizzy. I couldn't understand what he said; he is beyond understanding."

Lao Tzu is bound to be beyond understanding if you try to understand him through formality; otherwise, he is simple. But for Confucius he is difficult, almost impossible to understand, because he sees through forms, and Lao Tzu has no form and no formality. Nameless, without any form, he lives in the infinite.

The greatest politeness is free of all formality.

Lao Tzu was sitting, Confucius was waiting for him to stand up. Who was really polite? Confucius waiting for Lao Tzu to stand up, and welcome him and receive him because he is older, is just egoistic. Now the ego has taken the form of age, seniority. But Confucius could not look directly into the eyes of Lao Tzu, because Lao Tzu was right. He was saying: We are of the same age. Really, we are the same. The same life flows in you that flows in me. You are not superior to me; I am not superior to you. There is no question of superiority and inferiority, and there is no question of seniority and juniority. There is no question; we are one.

If Confucius could have looked into the eyes, and seen that those eyes were divine . . . But a man whose own eyes are filled with laws, rules, regulations, formalities, is almost blind; he cannot see.

Perfect conduct is free of concern.

You conduct yourself well because you are concerned. You behave well because you are concerned.

Just the other day a man came to me. He said, "I would like to take the jump: I would like to become a disciple, but there is my family, my children are studying at college, and I have a great responsibility toward them."

He is concerned. He has a duty to fulfill but no love. Duty is concern; it thinks in terms of something that has to be done because it is expected, because "What will people say if I leave?" Who thinks about what people will say? The ego. "What will people say? So first let me fulfill my duties." I never tell anybody to leave, I never tell anybody to renounce, but I insist that one should not be in some relationship because of duty—because then the whole relationship is ugly.

One should be in a relationship because of love. Then this man would not say, "I have a duty to fulfill." He would say, "I cannot come right now. My children are growing, and I love them, and I am happy working for them." Then this will be a happiness. Now it is not a happiness, it is a burden.

When you carry a burden, when you turn even your love into a burden, you cannot be happy. And if you have turned your love into a burden, your prayer will also become a burden, your meditation will also become a burden. Then you will say, "Because of this guru, this master, I am caught, and now I have to do this." It will not come out of you, out of your totality; it will not be overflowing. Why be worried? If there is love, wherever you are, there is no burden. And if you love your children, even if you leave them they will understand. If you don't love your children, and you go on serving them, they will never understand. And they will know that these are just false things.

This is happening. People come to see me and they say, "I have worked my whole life, and nobody even feels thankful toward me." How can anybody feel thankful toward you? You were carrying them like a burden. Even small children understand well when love is there, and they understand well when you are just doing as a duty. Duty is ugly, duty is violent; it shows your concern, but it doesn't show your spontaneity. Says Chuang Tzu: *Perfect conduct is free of concern.* Whatsoever is done, is done out of love—then you are not honest because honesty pays, you are honest because honesty is lovely.

Perfect Wisdom Is Unplanned

A wise person lives moment to moment, never planning. Only ignorant people plan, and when ignorant people plan, what can they plan? They plan out of their ignorance. Unplanned, they would have been better off, because out of ignorance only ignorance arises; out of confusion, only greater confusion is born.

A wise person lives moment to moment, has no planning. Then life is just free like a cloud floating in the sky, not going to some goal, not determined. The person has no map for the future, lives without a map, moves without a map—because the real thing is not the goal; the real thing is the beauty of the movement. The real thing is not reaching, the real thing is the journey.

> Remember: the real thing is the journey, the very traveling. It is so beautiful, why bother about the goal?

Remember: the real thing is the journey, the very traveling. It is so beautiful, why bother about the goal? If you are too bothered about the goal, you will miss the journey. And the journey is life—the goal can only be death.

The journey is life, and it is an infinite journey. You have been on the move from the very beginning—if there was any beginning. Those who know say there was no beginning, so from no-beginning you have been on the move, to the no-end you will be on the move—and if you are goal-oriented, you will miss. The whole is the journey—the path, the endless path, never beginning, never ending.

There really is no goal—goal is created by the cunning mind. Where is this whole existence moving? Where? It is not going anywhere. It is simply going, and the going is so beautiful; that is why existence is unburdened. There is no plan, no goal, and no purpose. It is not a business. It is a play, a *leela*. Every moment is the goal.

Perfect wisdom is unplanned.

Perfect love is without demonstrations.

Demonstration is needed because love is not there. And the less you love, the more you demonstrate—when it is there, you don't demonstrate. When a husband comes home with some present for the wife, she will know that something is wrong: "He must have stepped out of line, he must have met another woman. Now this is the explanation, this is a substitute; otherwise, love is such a gift, no other gift is needed."

Not that love will not give presents, but love itself is such a present. What else can you give? What else is possible? But whenever the husband feels that something is wrong, he has to put it right. Everything has to be rearranged, balanced.

And this is the problem: women are so intuitive that they know immediately; your present cannot deceive them. They will understand that something has gone wrong, otherwise, why this present?

Whenever you demonstrate, you demonstrate your inner poverty. If your religion becomes a demonstration, you are not religious. If your meditation becomes a demonstration, you are not meditative. Because whenever the real exists, it is such a light, there is no need to demonstrate it. When your house is lighted, when there is a flame, you do not go to the neighbors and tell them, "Look, our house has a lamp." It is there!

But when your house is in darkness, you try to convince your neighbors that the light is there. Convincing them, you try to convince yourself that this is the real. Why do you want to demonstrate? Because if the other is convinced, his conviction, her conviction, will help you to be convinced.

I have heard:

Once Mulla Nasruddin had a beautiful house, but he got bored, as everybody gets bored. Whether it was beautiful or not made no difference; living in the same house every day, he got bored. The house was beautiful, with a big garden, acres of green land, swimming pool, everything. But he got bored, so he called a real estate agent and told him, "I want to sell it. I am fed up; this house has become a hell."

The next day an advertisement appeared in the morning papers; the real estate agent had put in a beautiful advertisement. Mulla Nasruddin read it again and again and he was

*so convinced that he phoned the agent: "Wait, I don't want
to sell it. Your advertisement has convinced me so deeply that
now I know that for my whole life I have been wanting this
house, looking for this very house."*

When you can convince others of your love, you yourself
become convinced. But if you have love, there is no need—you
know.

When you have wisdom, there is no need to demonstrate it.
But when you have only knowledge, you demonstrate it. You
convince others, and when they are convinced, you are convinced
that you are a person of knowledge. When you have wisdom,
there is no need. If not a single person is convinced, even then
you are convinced; you alone are enough proof.

Perfect Sincerity Offers No Guarantee

All guarantees are because of insincerity. You guarantee, you
promise, you say: "This is the guarantee; I will do this." While
you are giving the guarantee, at that very moment the insincerity
is there.

Perfect sincerity offers no guarantee because perfect sincerity is so aware, aware of so many things. First, the future is
unknown. How can you make a guarantee? Life changes every
moment; how can you promise? All guarantees, all promises can
be only for this moment, not for the next. For the next moment
nothing can be done; you will have to wait.

If you are really sincere and you love a woman, you cannot say, "I will love you for my whole life." If you say this, you are a liar. This guarantee is false. But if you love, this moment is enough. The woman will not ask for your whole life: if love is there this moment, it is so fulfilling that one moment is enough for many lives. A single moment of love is eternity; she will not ask.

But if she is always asking, it is because in this moment, there is no love. So she asks, "What is the guarantee? Will you love me always?" This moment there is no love, and she is asking for a guarantee. This moment there is no love, and you guarantee for the future—because only through that guarantee can you deceive in this moment. You can create a beautiful picture of the future, and you can hide the ugly picture of the present. You say, "Yes, I will love you forever and forever. Even death will not part us."

What nonsense! What insincerity! How can you do this? You can do this, and you do it so easily, because you are not aware of what you are saying. The next moment is unknown; where it will lead, no one knows. What will happen, no one knows; no one can know it. Unknowability is part of the future game.

How can you guarantee? At the most you can say, "I love you this moment, and this moment I feel"—this is a feeling of this moment—"that even death cannot part us. But this is a feeling of this moment. This is not a guarantee. This moment, I feel like saying that I will love you always and always—but this is a feeling of this moment; this is no guarantee. What will happen in the future, nobody knows. We never knew this moment was coming, so how can we know about other moments? We will have to wait.

We will have to be prayerful that it happens, that I love you for ever and ever. But this is not a guarantee."

Perfect sincerity cannot give any guarantee. Perfect sincerity is so sincere that it cannot promise. It gives whatsoever it can give, here and now. Perfect sincerity lives in the present; it has no idea of the future. Mind moves in the future; being lives here and now. And perfect sincerity belongs to the being, not to the mind.

> Perfect sincerity cannot give any guarantee. Perfect sincerity is so sincere that it cannot promise.

Love, truth, meditation, sincerity, simplicity, innocence—all belong to the being. The opposites belong to the mind, and to hide the opposites, the mind creates false coins: false sincerity, which guarantees, promises; false love, which is just a name for duty; false beauty, which is just a face to cover inner ugliness. Mind creates false coins—and nobody is deceived, remember, except yourself.

Enough for today.

2

Guilt, Sin, and Repentance

Religions have made much fuss about repentance. Jesus goes on repeating again and again to his people, "Repent, repent, because the kingdom of God is close! Repent, because the day of judgment is coming close!"

First, religions make you feel guilty; otherwise, repentance would not have any relevance. You looked at a beautiful woman passing by, and there was a longing in you; your heart started beating faster. But you are married and the father of half a dozen children; moreover, you are a Christian. It does not suit you. You start feeling guilty; you have not done anything, but you start feeling guilty. Now, how to get rid of this guilt?

You are feeling guilty toward your wife, so you will have to bring ice cream—that is repentance. And the wife also understands it, that you must have done something wrong; otherwise, why ice cream? You have to bring toys to the children—that is repentance. But this is not enough. You have to go to the priest to confess that a beautiful woman was passing, and you had a sexual desire arise in you: "It is not right. Ask God's forgiveness on my behalf." Now you will be at ease. But you have not done anything, and you are unnecessarily wasting money on ice cream, toys, going to the priest—and becoming a victim of the priest, because now you will be always under his power.

The Catholic religion has more power over its people than any other religion, for the simple reason that everybody has to confess their sins. Naturally, the priest knows so much about everyone . . . you cannot leave the fold—he can expose you! Confession is being used to keep you in bondage; you cannot leave the fold.

The idea given to you is that this is how you repent, but the reality is that in most of the cases you are not committing any sin. To look at a beautiful woman and feel your heart beating faster is absolutely right, it is according to nature. It is respectful to the woman. In a better, more human society, where all these dead religions are finished, you would rather go to the woman and thank her for her beauty, to be grateful that she is alive. You don't feel guilty when you see a beautiful roseflower, you don't feel guilty when you see a beautiful sunset—then why should you feel guilty when you see a beautiful woman or a man? Beauty is not sin. It should be respected. And in a more intelligent, understanding, human world, the other person will accept your compliment with gratitude. You are not doing any harm.

Most of your sins are not sins at all. A few perhaps are mistakes, but not sins.

In my way of life, the word "sin" does not exist. You will be surprised to know that the original root, from where the word sin comes, means "forgetfulness."

That's great, that's what it should mean! You were not aware, you forgot; you committed a mistake. The idea of sin is invented by the priests to suppress you, subjugate you, humiliate you, destroy your dignity.

But forgetfulness is understandable. You can do something without being aware of what you are doing; later on, you become alert that you have done something wrong. Then the best way is not to go to the priest, but to go to the person to whom you have done the wrong. What business has the priest in it? And what business has God in it? The person whom you have harmed in any way—you should go to that person to ask forgiveness. That will be beautiful, and that will bring people together.

> In my way of life, the word "sin" does not exist. You will be surprised to know that the original root, from where the word sin comes, means "forgetfulness."

Hindus have an even simpler method. Every year go to the Ganges, have a good bath, and all your sins are washed away. Why make such small installment payments—once a week? Why not once a year? And if you cannot manage once a year, then every twelve years there is a special fair in Allahabad—perhaps the biggest gathering of people in the whole world, millions of people. Whatever you have done in twelve years, by taking a bath in the Ganges on that day, you are clean, free to do the same things again. At least for another twelve years, there is no problem.

In the West with Christianity, sin became the center. They say it is not because you are ignorant that you commit sin: you sin, that's why you are ignorant. The sin takes a primary significance. And not only is it your sin, it is the original sin of humanity! So you are burdened with a concept of sin: it creates guilt, it creates tension.

That's why Christianity could really not develop meditative techniques. It developed only prayer—because against sin, what can you do? You can be moral and prayerful. Nothing like the Ten Commandments exists in the East; there is no too-moralistic concept there, so the problems of people are different. For people coming from the West, guilt is their problem: deep down they feel guilty. Even those who have revolted, deep down they feel guilt. So it is more a psychological problem, concerned with the mind, and less concerned with the being. Their guilt has to be released. That's why the West had to develop psychoanalysis or confession. They were not developed in the East because they were never needed.

In the West, you have to confess, only then can you be free from the guilt deep down. Or you have to go through psychoanalysis, a long process of thought association, so the guilt is thrown out. But it is never thrown out permanently. It will come again because the concept of sin remains. It will be created again; it will accumulate again. So psychoanalysis can only be a temporary help, and confession is also a temporary help. You have to confess again and again. These are temporary helps against something that has been accepted: the root of the disease has been accepted.

In the East, it is not a question of psychology, it is a question of being. It is not a question of mental health; rather, it is a question of spiritual growth. You have to grow spiritually, to be more aware of things. You have not to change your basic behavior but to change your basic consciousness. Then the behavior follows.

So, Christianity is more behavioristic, and in that way it is defective because behavior is just the periphery. The question is not of what you *do*, the question is of what you *are*. So if you go on changing your doings, *you* are not changing. And, you can remain the same in a quite contrary doing—you can be a saint and still carry the same being as the sinner. Because doing can be changed very easily, it can be forced. So whosoever is coming from the West, their problem is of behavior, guilt. And I struggle with them just to make them aware of a deeper problem, which is of being, not of the psyche.

. . . The whole world has become a great crowd of "sinners" because everything has been condemned—everything. There is not a single thing you can do that has not been condemned by someone or other. With everything condemned, you become a sinner. Then guilt arises—and when there is guilt, you can pray, but the prayer is poisonous; it comes out of your guilt. When you are guilty, you can pray, but that prayer is based on fear. That prayer is not love, cannot be. Through guilt, love is impossible. Feeling yourself condemned, a sinner, how can you love?

This creation of a guilt complex was needed for the religions, not for you. Their business can continue only if they create guilt in you.

The whole business of religion depends on the guilt feelings that they can create in the masses. Churches, temples, religions, exist on your guilt. God has not created them; your guilt has created them. When you feel guilty, you need a priest to confess to. When you feel guilty, you need someone to lead you, to purify you. When you feel guilty, you have lost your center—now somebody can lead you.

> The whole business of religion depends on the guilt feelings that they can create in the masses.

And you can become part of a crowd only when you are not yourself. So you belong to Christianity or Hinduism or Mohammedanism. These "belongings" are simply guilt feelings. You cannot be alone. You are so guilty you cannot rely on yourself, you cannot depend on yourself—you cannot be independent. Somebody, some great organization, some cult, creed, is needed, so you can hide under its blanket and you can forget your guilt. Or you need some savior, you need someone who can suffer for your sins. This is just absurd.

Neither the Ganges nor God Can Forgive You

You will be surprised that in Thailand there is a small tribe of very primitive people who, even if in their dreams they harm somebody—for example, if they beat somebody in their dreams—

the first thing in the morning, they have to go to that person and ask forgiveness because even though it was a dream there must have been some desire somewhere which created the dream.

They tell the person, "I have not hurt you, and I am not going to ever hurt you. I have never been even aware that there is a desire to hurt you, but there must have been, because dreams are part of reality. They just don't come from nowhere."

And you will be surprised to know that that small tribe is the most peaceful tribe in the whole world: no fight, no rape, no murder, no suicide. And for thousands of years they have been following the same way. Slowly, slowly they have stopped dreaming too. They have become so innocent that even in the unconscious there are no longer any desires to be violent, to be a rapist, to torture somebody, to kill somebody.

In thousands of years, continually going to the man and asking for his forgiveness—and he is amazed, because he knows of nothing that you have done to him. But it brings you closer to him—he hugs you, he says, "There is nothing to be worried about, it was only a dream."

But you insist, "It does not matter that it was only a dream; it was my dream. I am involved in it, and unless you forgive me, I will suffer."

If a man like Sigmund Freud had gone to Thailand to these people, he would have been amazed that his psychoanalysis is of no use. They don't have any dreams; you cannot psychoanalyze them. Once in a while somebody may have a dream, but they have found a way to get rid of even a slight unconscious desire.

There is no question of sin in your life. You can, at the most, commit a mistake; you can do something you never wanted to do, and then there is heaviness on your heart. Then do something to undo what you have committed.

. . . I am not teaching you a religion. I simply want to tell you the truth. If you have done something wrong, go to the person. Be humble, ask their forgiveness. Only that person can forgive you, nobody else—neither the Ganges nor God.

And remember the meaning of the word *sin*: forgetfulness. So now, don't forget again and do the same; otherwise, your asking forgiveness becomes meaningless.

Now be careful, be alert, be conscious, and don't do the same thing again. That is true repentance. Once, you made the mistake—it was just a mistake. To err is human; there is nothing to be worried about.

. . .

Nothing Cleanses Like Repentance

Jesus said:
I took my stand in the midst of the world, and in flesh I appeared to them.
I found them all drunk; I found none of them athirst.
And my soul was afflicted for the sons of men because they are blind in their heart and they do not see that empty they have come into the world, and empty they seek to go out of the world again.

But now they are drunk. When they have shaken off their wine, then they will repent.

Jesus said: If the flesh has come into existence because of the spirit, it is a marvel; but if the spirit has come into existence because of the body, it is a marvel of marvels. But I marvel at how this great wealth has made its home in this poverty.

—from "The Gospel of Thomas"

Jesus or Buddha or anybody who is awakened will find you all drunk. The drunkenness is of many types, but the drunkenness is there. You are not alert, you are not awake: you simply think that you are awake and alert. Your sleep continues from birth to death.

Gurdjieff used to tell a small story:

There was a man who owned thousands of sheep, and he was always in trouble because the sheep would go astray, and they would become the victims of wild animals. So he asked a wise man, and the wise man suggested, "Keep watchdogs." So he had a hundred dogs to keep watch on the sheep. They would not allow the sheep to go out, and if any sheep tried to go out, they would kill it.

By and by they became so addicted to killing that they started to murder the sheep; they became a danger. So again the man came to the wise man and said, "It has become dangerous; the protectors have become murderers."

It always happens: look at your politicians, they are the protectors, the watchdogs, but once they are powerful, they start killing.

The wise man said, "Then there is only one way. I will come." So he came, and he hypnotized all the sheep and told them, "You are awake, alert, completely free. Nobody is your owner." Then those sheep remained in that hypnotic state, and they would not go anywhere. They would not escape because this was not a prison, and they all believed that they were the owners, masters of their own selves. Even if a sheep was killed by the master, they would think, "This is her fate, not mine. Nobody can kill me. I have an immortal self, and I am totally free, so there is no need to escape." Then there was no need for watchdogs, and the master was at ease because the sheep were hypnotized, they lived in a semi-sleep.

And that is the state in which you are, in which Jesus finds you, in which I find you. But nobody has hypnotized you; this is an autohypnosis. You are both the wise man who hypnotized the sheep and the sheep who was hypnotized; you are autohypnotized.

There is a certain method of autohypnotizing yourself: if you think a particular thought continuously, you will be hypnotized by it; if you look at a thing continuously, you will be hypnotized by it; if you brood on something continuously, you will be hypnotized by it. Where you move is not the question, because you carry your mind with you, and your mind goes on creating a world around you. Somebody is hypnotized through sex, somebody is hypnotized through wealth, somebody is hypnotized through power, but everybody is hypnotized. And nobody has done this to you—you have been doing this yourself, it is your work. But you have been doing it so long that you have completely forgotten that you are both the magician and the sheep.

Once a person realizes "I am the magician and I am the sheep," then things start changing because then the first spark of transformation has entered. Now you can never be the same again because the hypnosis has started to drop. A breaking point has come; something of awareness has entered you.

You may have different objects of hypnosis: find out which is the object of your hypnosis, which one attracts you most, which one has become the focal point of your being, and then look at it, at how you got hypnotized by it. Repetition is the method of hypnosis: looking at anything continuously or thinking about it continuously. If you go to a hypnotist, he will say, "You are falling asleep, falling asleep, falling asleep, falling asleep." He will go on repeating the same thing in a monotonous voice, and soon you will be fast asleep. He was not doing anything but simply repeating something. Hearing it again and again and again, you will fall asleep; you have hypnotized yourself.

Remember this, because you are doing this continuously, and it is being done by society continuously. The whole mechanism of propaganda consists of repetitions. Politicians go on repeating certain things. They go on repeating them, and they don't bother whether you listen or not. Listening is not the point, because if they just go on repeating, by and by you are convinced, persuaded, not logically, not rationally—they never argue with you—but just through repetition you are hypnotized.

Hitler went on repeating that the Jews were the reason for the misery and fall of Germany: "Once the Jews are destroyed, there will be no problem. You are the owners of the whole world; you are a special race. You have come here to dominate; you are the master race."

Even his friends never believed it in the beginning, and he himself never believed it in the beginning because this was such a patent lie. But as he continued, by and by people started believing in it: they were hypnotized. And when other people were hypnotized by it, he too was hypnotized into thinking that there must be some truth in it: "When millions of people believe it, there must be something true in it." Then his friends started believing it, then it became a mutual hypnosis, and then the whole of Germany got into it.

> Hitler has written in his autobiography, *Mein Kampf*, that there is a simple process for transforming a lie into a truth: just go on repeating it.

One of the most intelligent races behaved very foolishly. Why? What happened to the German mind?—just repetition, propaganda.

Hitler has written in his autobiography, *Mein Kampf*, that

there is a simple process for transforming a lie into a truth: just go on repeating it. And he knew from his own experience. If you go on repeating a particular thing—you smoke, you go on smoking every day—it becomes a hypnosis. Then, even if you come to know that it is useless, futile, foolish, dangerous to health, nothing can be done, because now it is an autohypnosis. A person goes on overeating. He knows it is bad—he suffers because of it, he is continuously ill—but still, when he sits down to eat he cannot help it. It is compulsive. What is compulsion? Because he has been doing it so long he has become hypnotized by it. He is drunk.

Mulla Nasruddin came home one night very late; it must have been three in the morning. He knocked; his wife was very angry, but Mulla said, "Wait! First give me one minute to explain, then you can start. I was sitting with a very sick friend."

His wife said, "A very likely story! But tell me the name of the friend."

Nasruddin thought and thought and thought, and then he said triumphantly, "He was so sick he couldn't tell me!"

The mind, if it is drunk, may find excuses, but all those excuses are false, just like this one: "The friend was so sick that he couldn't tell me." For sex you will find excuses, for smoking you will find excuses, for your lust for power you will find excuses, but all excuses are lame. The real fact is that you are not ready to recognize that it has become compulsive, that you are under an obsession, you are under a hypnosis.

This is what a Jesus finds: everyone drunk and fast asleep. You cannot find it because you yourself are asleep. Unless you are awake, you cannot become aware of what is happening all around. The whole world is moving in a somnambulism. That's why there is so much misery, so much violence, so much war. It is unnecessary, but it has to be so because people who are asleep and drunk cannot be responsible for anything. If somebody came to Jesus to ask what he should do to change, Jesus would say: You cannot do anything to change unless you become awake. What can you do? What can a man who is fast asleep do to change his dreams? What can he do?

People would come with the same question to Gurdjieff—and Gurdjieff is the man most representative of Jesus in our age, not the Vatican pope. Gurdjieff is the most representative because he believed in, and worked out, the same method of friction that Jesus was working with. He created many types of crosses for people to hang themselves on and be transformed. Gurdjieff also used to say that you cannot do anything unless you *are*. And if you are not awake, you are not there, you simply believe that you are. This belief won't help.

Now look at these sayings. They are all very profound, deep, very significant, and can become guide-lights on your path. Remember them.

Jesus said:

I took my stand in the midst of the world, and in flesh I appeared to them.

I found them all drunk; I found none of them athirst.

Jesus never renounced the world; he was standing in the midst of us all. He was not an escapist; he moved in the marketplace, he lived with the crowd. He talked to prostitutes, laborers, farmers, fishermen. He didn't go out of the world; he remained here amidst you. He knew the world better than anybody who has escaped from it.

It is no wonder that Christ's message became so powerful. Mahavira's message never became so powerful, but Jesus converted almost half of the world. Why?—because he remained in the world; he understood the world, its ways, the people, the mind. He moved with them, he came to know how they function—asleep, drunk—and he started to find ways and means to awaken them.

On the last night, when Jesus was caught—or managed to be caught—when the last drama was enacted, a disciple was with him. And Jesus said, "This is my last night, so I will go into deep prayer. I have to pray, and you are to keep vigil. Don't fall asleep! I will come back and see . . . and this is my last night, remember!"

Jesus went, and after half an hour he came back again. The disciple was fast asleep. He awakened him and told him, "You are fast asleep, and I told you to keep vigil because this is my last night. Remain alert because I will not be here again! Then you can sleep for ever and ever. But with me . . . at least on my last night remain alert!"

The disciple said, "Excuse me, I was feeling so sleepy that I couldn't help it. But I will try now."

Jesus went again into prayer. After half an hour he was back, and again the disciple was fast asleep. He awakened him again and said, "What are you doing? The morning is coming near, and I will be caught!"

The disciple said, "Excuse me, forgive me, but the flesh is very strong, and the will is very weak, and the body was so heavy, and I thought, 'What is wrong in taking a little sleep? A little sleep, and by the time he comes back, I will be awake again.'"

Jesus came a third time, and the disciple was fast asleep. But this is the situation of all disciples. Sleepiness has become just second nature. What does sleepiness mean? It means that you are not aware that you are; then whatsoever you do is irresponsible. You are mad, and whatsoever you do, you do just like a drunkard.

Says Jesus:

I took my stand in the midst of the world, and in flesh I appeared to them.

I appeared in the flesh to them—I was in the body, they could see me, they could hear me, they could feel me—but still they missed. They missed because . . . *I found them all drunk.* They were not there really, no consciousness at all. I knocked at their doors, but they were not at home.

If Jesus comes to your home and knocks, will you be there to receive him? You will be somewhere else; you are never at home. You go on wandering all over the world, except to your home.

> Where is your home? Inside you, where the center of consciousness is, is your home.

Where is your home? Inside you, where the center of consciousness is, is your home. You are never there, because only in deep meditation are you there. And when you are deep in meditation you can immediately recognize Jesus; whether he comes in the body or bodiless makes no difference. If you are at home, you will recognize the knock. But if you are not at home, what can be done? Jesus will knock, and you will not be there. That is the meaning of the word *drunk*: not at home.

Really, whenever you want to forget yourself you take alcohol, drugs; whenever you want to forget yourself you drink. Drinking means forgetfulness, and the whole of religion consists of remembering; hence, all religions insist against drinking. Not that there is something wrong in drinking in itself; if you are not moving on the path there is nothing wrong in it. But if you are moving on the path, then there cannot be anything more wrong than that, because the whole path consists of self-remembering, and drinking is forgetfulness.

But why do you want to forget yourself? Why are you so bored with yourself? Why can't you live with yourself? Why can't you be alert and at ease? What is the problem? The problem is that whenever you are alert, alone, you feel empty; you feel as if you are nobody. You feel a nothingness inside, and that nothingness becomes the abyss. You get scared, you start running from it.

Deep inside you, you are an abyss, and that's why you go on escaping. Buddha called that abyss no-self, *anatta*. There is nobody inside. When you look, it is a vast expansion, but nobody is there: just inner sky, an infinite abyss, endless, beginningless. The moment you look you get dizzy, you start running, you immediately escape. But where can you escape to? Wherever you go, that emptiness will be with you because it is you. It is your Tao, your nature. One has to come to terms with it.

Meditation is nothing but coming to terms with your inner emptiness: recognizing it, not escaping; living through it, not escaping; being through it, not escaping. Then suddenly the emptiness becomes the fullness of life. When you don't escape from it, it is the most beautiful thing, the purest, because only emptiness can be pure. If something is there, dirt has entered; if something is there, then death has entered; if something is there, then limitation has entered. If something is there, then godliness cannot be there. Godliness means the great abyss, the ultimate abyss. It is there, but you are never trained to look into it.

> Meditation is nothing but coming to terms with your inner emptiness: recognizing it, not escaping; living through it, not escaping; being through it, not escaping.

It is just like when you go to the hills and look into the valley: you get dizzy. Then you don't want to look because a fear grips you; you may fall. But no hill is so high and no valley so deep as the valley that exists inside you. And whenever you look inside you feel a dizziness, nausea; you immediately escape, you close your eyes and start running. You have been running for millions of lives, but you have not reached anywhere; you cannot.

One has to come to terms with the inner emptiness. And once you come to terms with it, suddenly the emptiness changes its nature: it becomes the all. Then it is not empty, not negative; it is the most positive thing in existence. But acceptance is the door.

That's why there is so much attraction for alcohol, LSD, marijuana, drugs. And there are many types of drugs: physical, chemical, mental; wealth, power, politics—everything is a drug.

Look at a politician: he is drugged; he is drunk with power; he does not walk on the earth. Look at a man of wealth: you think he walks on the earth? No, his feet never touch the earth; he is very high; he has wealth. Only poor men walk on the earth, only beggars; a rich man flies in the sky. When you fall in love with a woman, suddenly you are on high; suddenly you never again walk on the earth. A romance has entered; the whole quality of your being is different because now you are drunk. Sex is the deepest alcohol that nature has given to you.

Jesus said:

I found them all drunk; I found none of them athirst.

This has to be understood, a very delicate point: if you are drunk with this world, you cannot be thirsty for the other. If you are drunk with ordinary alcohol, with ordinary wine, you cannot be thirsty for the divine wine—impossible! When you are not drunk with this world, a thirst arises. And that thirst cannot be fulfilled by anything that belongs to this world. Only the unknown can fulfill it; only the invisible can fulfill it.

So Jesus says a very contradictory thing: *I found them all drunk; I found none of them athirst.* Nobody was thirsty because they thought they had already found the key, the treasure, the kingdom. So then there was no search.

Godliness is a drunkenness of a different type. Kabir has said: "*Aisi tari lagi*: I have fallen into such a drunkenness that nothing now can disturb it, it is eternal." Ask Omar Khayyam: he knows, he talks about the wine of the other world. And Fitzgerald totally misunderstood him, because he is not talking of the wine that you can get here; he is talking of the divine wine, which is the Sufi symbol for God. Once you are drunk with godliness, then there will be no thirst at all.

But this world and its wine can give you only temporary relief, can give you only temporary gaps of forgetfulness. And the difference is diametrical: when someone is drunk with the wine of godliness, he is totally alert, aware, fully conscious. When somebody is drunk with this world and its wines, he is hypnotized, asleep, moves in a slumber, lives in a sleep; his whole life is a long dream.

I found them all drunk; I found none of them athirst.

And my soul was afflicted for the sons of men, because they are blind in their heart and they do not see that empty they have come into the world, and empty they seek to go out of the world again.

And my soul was afflicted . . . You cannot understand what suffering happens to a Jesus or a Buddha when he looks at you, drunk with this world, not thirsty at all for the divine, for the truth. Living in lies, and believing in lies as if they were truths—and missing, for nothing, missing all for nothing. Then it happens that the smallest things can become barriers.

Once it happened that a man was very ill. The illness was that he continually felt that his eyes were popping out and his ears were continually ringing. By and by he became crazy because it went on twenty-four hours a day. He couldn't sleep; he couldn't do his work.

So he consulted doctors. One doctor suggested, "Remove the appendix," so the appendix was removed, but nothing happened. Another suggested, "Remove all the teeth," so all his teeth were removed. Nothing happened; the man simply became old, that's all. Then somebody suggested that the tonsils should be removed. There are millions of advisers, and if you start listening to them, they will kill you. So his tonsils were removed, but nothing happened. Then he consulted the greatest doctor known.

The doctor diagnosed, and he said, "Nothing can be done because the cause cannot be found. At the most you can live six months more. And I must be frank with you, because all that could be done has been done. Now nothing can be done."

The man came out of the doctor's office and thought, "If I only have six months to live, then why not live well?" He was a miser, and he had never lived, so he ordered the latest and biggest car; he purchased a beautiful bungalow. He ordered thirty suits; he even ordered shirts to be made to order.

He went to the tailor, who measured him and said, "Size thirty-six sleeves, sixteen collar."

The man said, "No, fifteen collar, because I always wear a fifteen."

The tailor measured again and said, "Sixteen!"

The man said, "But I have always worn a fifteen!"

The tailor said, "Okay then, have it your own way, but I tell you, if you wear a fifteen-inch collar, you will have popping eyes and ringing in the ears!"

You are missing the divine—and not for very great causes, no! Just a size fifteen collar, and the eyes cannot see, they are popping out of their sockets, and the ears cannot hear, they are ringing.

The cause of man's illness is simple, because he is addicted to small things. The things of this world are very small. Even if you get a kingdom, what is it?—a very small thing. Where are the kingdoms that existed in history? Where is Babylon? Where is Assyria? Where is the kingdom of the Pharaoh? They all disappeared, just ruins; and those kingdoms were great. But what was attained by them? What did Genghis Khan attain? What did Alexander the Great attain? All kingdoms are just trivial things.

And you don't know what you are missing; you are missing the kingdom of God. Even if you become successful, what will you get through it? Where will you get through it? Look at successful people, diagnose them: where have they reached? Look at people who sit on thrones of success: where have they reached? They are also in search of mental peace—more than you are. They are also afraid of death, and trembling, just like you.

If you look at your successful people minutely, you will find that they also have clay feet. Death will take them, and with death all success disappears, all fame disappears. The whole thing seems to be a nightmare: so much effort, so much misery, so much hardship, and nothing is gained. In the end, death comes and everything disappears like a bubble. And because of this bubble, that which is eternal is lost.

And my soul was afflicted for the sons of men, because they are blind in their heart, and they do not see that empty they have come into the world, and empty they seek to go out of the world again.

Empty you have come, but not exactly empty: filled with desires. Empty you will go, but not exactly empty: again filled with desires. But desires are dreams—you remain empty—they have nothing substantial in them. You are born empty, and then you move in the world and accumulate things, just believing that these things will give you fulfillment. You remain empty. Death snatches everything; you move again into the grave, again empty.

To what point does this whole life come? To what meaning and conclusion? What do you achieve through it? This is the affliction of a Jesus or a Buddha: looking at people, one can see they are blind. And why are they blind? Where is their blindness? It is not that they are not clever; they are too clever, more than they need. More than they can afford, more than is good for them. They are very clever, cunning. They think they are wise. It is not that they cannot see; they can see, but they can see only something that belongs to this world. Their heart is blind; their heart cannot see.

Can you see with your heart? Have you ever seen anything with your heart? Many times you may have thought, "The sun is rising and the morning is beautiful," and think it is from the heart. No, because your mind is still chattering, "The sun is beautiful, the morning is beautiful," and you may be simply repeating others' ideas. Have you really realized that the morning is beautiful: this morning, the phenomenon that is happening here? Or are you repeating words?

You go to a flower: have you really gone? Has the flower touched your heart? Has it reached to your deepest core of being? Or do you just look at the flower and say, "Good, it is beautiful, nice." These are words and almost dead, because they are not coming from the heart. No word ever comes from the heart; feeling comes, but no words. Words come from the head, feeling comes from the heart. But there we are blind. Why are we blind there?—because the heart leads into dangerous paths.

So nobody is allowed to live with the heart.

Your parents have taken care that you should live with the head, not with the heart, because the heart may lead you to failure in this world. It does lead to failure, and unless you fail in this world you will not be athirst for the other. The head leads to success in this world. It is cunning, calculating, it is a manipulator; it leads you to success. So every school, every college and university teaches you how to be more "heady," how to be more "headfull." And those who are headfull get the gold medals. They are successful, and then they have the keys to enter into this world.

> Your parents have taken care that you should live with the head, not with the heart, because the heart may lead you to failure in this world.

But the person with heart will be a failure, because they cannot exploit. They will be so loving that they cannot exploit. They will be so loving that he cannot be a miser, an accumulator. They will be so loving that they will go and share, and whatsoever they have they will give, rather than snatching things from people. The person with heart will be a failure and will be so true that they cannot deceive you. They will be sincere and honest, authentic—but then will be a stranger in this world, where only cunning people can succeed. That is why every parent takes care that before the child moves into the world, his heart should become blind, completely closed.

You cannot pray, you cannot love. Can you? Can you pray? You can pray: go into a church on Sunday; people are praying—but everything is false; even their prayer comes from their heads. They have learned it, it is not from the heart. Their hearts are empty, dead, they don't feel a thing. People "love"—they get married, and children are born to them—not out of love; everything is out of calculation, everything is out of arithmetic. You are afraid of love because no one knows where love will lead you. No one knows the ways of the heart; they are mysterious. With the head you are on the right path, on the highway; with the heart you move into the jungle. There are no roads, no road signs; you have to find the path yourself.

With the heart you are individual, solitary. With the head you are part of the society. The head has been trained by the society, it is part of the society. With the heart you become solitary, an outsider. So every society takes care to kill the heart, and Jesus says:

. . . because they are blind in their hearts and do not see that empty they have come into the world, and empty they seek to go out of the world again.

Only the heart can see how empty you are. What have you gained? What maturity, what growth has happened to you? What ecstasy has come to you? No benediction yet? The whole past has been a rotten thing. And in the future you are going to repeat the past: what else can you do? This is the affliction of a Jesus, of a Buddha. He feels miserable for you.

But now they are drunk. When they have shaken off their wine, then they will repent.

This is about you. Don't think "they"—"they" means "you." When you are shaken out of your drunkenness, you will repent.

This word *repent* became very meaningful. The whole of Christianity depends on repentance; no other religion has depended so much on repentance.

Repentance is beautiful if it comes through the heart, if you realize, "Yes, Jesus is right, we have wasted our lives." This wasting is the sin—not that Adam committed the sin—this wasting of your life, of the possibility, the potentiality, the opportunity to grow and become God-like or become gods, wasting this time, wasting it with futile things, collecting useless junk. And when you become aware, you will repent. And if this repentance comes through the heart, it will cleanse you. Nothing cleanses like repentance. And this is one of the most beautiful things in Christianity.

In Hinduism there is no teaching about repentance; they have not worked out that key at all. This is unique to Christianity. If you repent totally, if it comes from the heart, if you cry and weep, if your whole being feels and repents that you have been wasting the opportunity given by existence, you have not been grateful, you have misbehaved, you have mistreated your own being . . . you feel the sin.

This is the sin! Not that you have murdered somebody or that you have stolen something; that is nothing. Those are minor sins, which are born out of this original sin: that you have been drunk. You open your eyes, your heart is filled with repentance, and then a scream, a cry, comes out of your being. There is no need for words, you need not say to God, "I repent, forgive me." No need—your whole being becomes a repentance. Suddenly, you are cleansed of all the past. This is one of the most secret keys that Jesus delivered to the world.

Jainas say that you have to work it out, it is a long process: whatsoever you have done in the past has to be undone. If you have done a wrong in the past, it has to be undone. It is mathematical: if you have committed a sin, you have to do something to balance it. And Hindus say that you have committed such sin, that you are in such ignorance—so many actions out of ignorance— and the past is so vast that it is not easy to get out of it. Many more works will be needed, only then can you clean the past.

But Jesus has given a beautiful key. He says: "Just repent and the whole past is washed clean." It seems to be a very unbelievable thing because how can it happen? And that is the difference between Hindus, Buddhists, Jainas, and Christianity. Hindus,

Buddhists, and Jainas can never believe that can happen just by repentance, because they don't know what repentance is. Jesus worked it out. It is one of the oldest keys.

But understand what repentance is. Just saying the words won't do, and saying them halfheartedly won't do. When your whole being repents—your whole being throbs, and you feel it in every pore, every fiber, that you have done wrong, and you have done wrong because you have been drunk, and now you repent—suddenly there is a transformation. The past disappears, and the projection of the future from the past disappears; you are thrown to here and now, you are thrown to your own being. And for the first time you feel the inner nothingness. It is not empty in a negative sense, it is just that the temple is so vast, like space . . .

You are forgiven, Jesus says; you are forgiven if you repent.

Jesus's master was John the Baptist. His whole teaching was, "Repent because the day of judgment is near!" This was his whole teaching. He was a very wild man, a great revolutionary, and he went from one corner of his country to another, with just one message: "Repent because the last judgment is very near." That is why Christians completely dropped the theory of rebirth. Not that Jesus was not aware of rebirth: he knew, he knew well that there is a cycle of continuous rebirths, but he completely dropped the idea just to give repentance totality.

If there are many lives, your repentance cannot be total. You can wait, you can postpone. You can think, "If I have missed in this life, nothing is wrong. The next life . . ." That's what Hindus have been doing—they are the laziest people in the world because of this theory. And the theory is right, that is the problem; they can always postpone—there is no hurry. Why be in such a hurry? That's why Hindus have never bothered about time. They never invented watches, and, left to themselves, they would not invent them. So a watch, for a Hindu mind, is really a foreign element: a clock in a Hindu house doesn't suit.

The clock is a Christian invention because time is short, running fast. It is not a clock, it is life running fast out of your hands. This death is going to be the final one; you cannot postpone. Just to avoid postponement, Jesus and John the Baptist—who was his master, who initiated Jesus into the mysteries—their whole teaching depends on it: "Repent! For there is no more time left, don't postpone any further because then you will be lost." They bring the whole thing to an intensity.

If I suddenly say, "This is going to be the last day, and tomorrow the world is going to disappear, the bomb is to be dropped," and then I say: "Repent!"—then your total being will be focused, centered, you will be here and now. And then there will come a scream, a cry, a wild scream from your being. It will not be in words; it will be more existential than that: it will be from the heart. Not only will your eyes weep, but your heart will be filled with tears, your whole being will be filled with tears: you have missed.

If this repentance happens—this is an intensity of becoming alert—all the past is cleaned.

No need to undo it. No, because it has never been a reality. It was a dream; no need to undo it, just become alert. And with the sleep, all the dreams and nightmares disappear. They have never been there in reality in the first place; they have been your thoughts. And don't be lazy about it, because you have been postponing for many lives. You can postpone for many more: postponement is such an attraction for the mind. The mind always says, "tomorrow"—always. Tomorrow is the shelter. Tomorrow is the shelter of all sin, and virtue arises at this moment.

Start with Yourself

If you are feeling miserable, let it become a meditation. Sit silently, close the doors. First feel the misery with as much intensity as possible. Feel the hurt.

Somebody has insulted you—now, the best way to avoid the hurt is to go and insult that person. So you become occupied with that person—that is not meditation.

If somebody has insulted you, feel thankful that they have given you an opportunity to feel a deep wound. They have opened a wound in you—the wound may be created by many, many insults that you have suffered in your whole life. This person may not be the cause of all the suffering, but they have triggered a process.

Just close your room, sit silently, with no anger for the person but with total awareness of the feeling that is arising in you—the hurt feeling that you have been rejected, that you have been insulted. And then you will be surprised that not only is this person there, all the men and all the women and all the people that have ever insulted you will start moving in your memory.

You will not only start remembering them, you will start reliving them. You will be going into a kind of primal—feel the hurt, feel the pain, don't avoid it. That's why, in many therapies, the patient is told not to take any drugs before the therapy begins, for the simple reason that drugs are a way to escape from your inner misery. They don't allow you to see your wounds, they repress them. They don't allow you to go into your suffering, and unless you go into your suffering, you cannot be released from the imprisonment of it.

It is perfectly scientific to drop all drugs before going into a therapy—if possible, even drugs like coffee, tea, smoking, because these are all ways to escape.

Have you watched? Whenever you feel nervous you immediately start smoking. It is a way to avoid nervousness; you become occupied with smoking. Really, it is a regression. Smoking makes you again feel like a child—unworried, un-responsible—because smoking is nothing but a symbolic breast. The hot smoke going in simply takes you back to the days when you were feeding on the mother's breast and the warm milk was going in; the nipple has now become the cigarette. The cigarette is a symbolic nipple.

Through regression you avoid the responsibilities and the pains of being adult. And that's what goes on through many, many drugs. Modern man is drugged as never before, because modern man is living in great suffering. Without drugs it will be impossible to live in so much suffering. Those drugs create a barrier; they keep you drugged, they don't allow you enough sensitivity to know your pain.

The first thing to do is close your doors and stop any kind of occupation—looking at the TV, listening to the radio, reading a book. Stop all occupation because that too is a subtle drug. Just be silent, utterly alone. Don't even pray, because that again is a drug: you are becoming occupied; you start talking to God; you start praying; you escape from yourself.

Just be yourself. Whatsoever the pain of it, and whatsoever the suffering of it, let it be so. First experience it in its total intensity. It will be difficult; it will be heartrending. You may start crying like a child; you may start rolling on the ground in deep pain; your body may go through contortions. You may suddenly become aware that the pain is not only in the heart, it is all over the body—that it is aching all over, that it is painful all over, that your whole body is nothing but pain.

If you can experience it—this is of tremendous importance— then start absorbing it. Don't throw it away. It is such a valuable energy, don't throw it away. Absorb it, drink it, accept it, welcome it. Feel grateful to it. And say to yourself, "This time I'm not going to avoid it; this time I'm not going to reject it; this time I'm not going to throw it away. This time I will drink it and receive it like a guest. This time I will digest it."

It may take a few days for you to be able to digest it, but the day it happens, you have stumbled upon a door that will take you really far, far away. A new journey has started in your life: you are moving into a new kind of being—because immediately, the moment you accept the pain with no rejection anywhere, its energy and its quality changes. It is no longer pain. In fact, one is simply surprised—one cannot believe it, it is so incredible. One cannot believe that suffering can be transformed into ecstasy, that pain can become joy.

But in ordinary life, you are aware that opposites are always joined together, that they are not opposites but complementaries. You know perfectly well your love can at any moment become hate, and your hate can at any moment become love. In fact, if you hate too much, intensely and totally, it is bound to become love.

That's what happened to the person called Saul, who later on became Paul and founded the ugly phenomenon of the Christian church. Jesus is not the founder of the Christian church—the founder of the Christian church is Saint Paul. And the story is worth remembering.

When he was born, his name was Saul. And he was so anti-Christ that his whole life was devoted to destroying Christians and Christianity. His whole dedication was to persecute Christians, destroying any possibility of Christianity for the future, and effacing the name of Christ. He must have hated tremendously; his hate cannot have been ordinary. When you devote your whole life to the object of your hatred, it is bound to be really total. Otherwise, who cares? If you hate something, you don't devote your whole life to it. But if you hate totally, then it becomes a life-and-death problem.

Persecuting Christians, destroying Christians, destroying their power-holds, arguing with Christians, convincing them that this was nonsense, that this man Jesus was mad, a neurotic, a pretender, a hypocrite—one day it happened, the miracle happened. Saul was going to persecute more Christians in another town. On the way he was alone, and suddenly he saw Jesus appearing out of nowhere and asking him, "Why do you persecute me?"

Out of shock, terror, he fell on the ground, apologizing, crying great tears of repentance. The vision disappeared, and with the disappearance of the vision, the old Saul disappeared. To remember this point, he changed his name to Paul—the old man was dead; a new man had arrived. And he became the founder of the Christian church. He became a great lover of Jesus, the greatest lover the world has ever known. Hate can become love.

Jesus did not appear; it was just the intensity of Saul's hate that projected Jesus. It was not Jesus who asked him, "Why do you persecute me?" It was his own unconscious, which was suffering so much because of this hatred of Jesus. It was his own unconscious that asked him, "Why do you persecute me?" It was his own unconscious that became personified in the vision of Jesus. The miracle happened because the hate was total.

Whenever anything is total, it turns into its opposite. This is a great secret to be remembered. Whenever something is total, it changes into its opposite because there is no way to go any further; you have arrived at the cul-de-sac.

Watch an old-world clock with a pendulum. It goes on and on: the pendulum goes to the left, to the extreme left, and then there is a point beyond which it cannot go, then it starts moving toward the right.

Opposites are complementaries. If you can suffer your suffering in totality, in great intensity, you will be surprised: Saul becomes Paul. You will not be able to believe it when it happens for the first time, that your own suffering absorbed willingly, welcomingly, becomes a great blessing. The same energy that becomes hate becomes love; the same energy that becomes pain becomes pleasure; the same energy that becomes suffering becomes bliss.

But start with your own self.

. . .

Be Grateful to All

The ordinary mind always throws the responsibility on somebody else. It is always the other making you suffer. Your wife is making you suffer; your husband is making you suffer; your parents are making you suffer; your children are making you suffer, or the financial system of the society—capitalism, communism, fascism, the prevalent political ideology, the social structure, or fate, karma, God . . . you name it.

People have millions of ways to shirk responsibility. But the moment you say somebody else—XYZ—is making you suffer, then you cannot do anything to change it. What can you do? When the society changes, and communism comes and there is a classless world, then everybody will be happy. Before that, it is not possible. How can you be happy in a society that is poor? And how can you be happy in a society that is dominated by the capitalists? How can you be happy with a society that is bureaucratic? How can you be happy with a society that does not allow you freedom?

Excuses and excuses and excuses—excuses just to avoid one single insight that "I am responsible for myself. Nobody else is responsible for me; it is absolutely and utterly my responsibility. Whatsoever I am, I am my own creation." Once this insight settles—"I am responsible for my life—for all my suffering, for my pain, for all that has happened to me and is happening to me—I have chosen it this way; these are the seeds that I sowed, and now I am reaping the crop; I am responsible"— once this insight becomes a natural understanding in you, then everything else is simple. Then life starts taking a new turn, starts moving into a new dimension. That dimen-

> Can anybody prevent you from dropping your misery, from transforming your misery into bliss? Nobody.

sion is conversion, revolution, mutation—because once I know I am responsible, I also know that I can drop it any moment I decide to. Nobody can prevent me from dropping it.

Can anybody prevent you from dropping your misery, from transforming your misery into bliss? Nobody. Even if you are in a jail, chained, imprisoned, nobody can imprison you; your soul still remains free. Of course you have a very limited situation, but even in that limited situation you can sing a song. You can either cry tears of helplessness or you can sing a song. Even with chains on your feet you can dance; then even the sound of the chains will have a melody to it.

And be grateful to everyone. Because everybody is creating a space for you to be transformed—even those who think they are obstructing you, even those whom you think are enemies. Your friends, your enemies, good people and bad people, favorable circumstances, unfavorable circumstances—all together they are creating the context in which you can be transformed and become a buddha. Be grateful to all.

A man once came and spat on Buddha, on his face. Of course his disciples were enraged. His closest disciple, Ananda, said to him, "This is too much!" He was red-hot with anger. He said to Buddha, "Just give me permission so that I can show this man what he has done."

Buddha wiped his face and said to the man, "Thank you, sir. You created a context in which I could see whether I can still be angry or not. And I am not, and I am tremendously happy. And also you created a context for Ananda: now he can see that he can still be angry. Many thanks—we are so grateful! Once in a while, please, you are invited to come. Whenever you have the urge to spit on somebody, you can come to us."

It was such a shock to the man, he could not believe his ears, what was happening. He had come expecting that he would anger Buddha. He had failed. The whole night he could not sleep; he tossed and turned and could not sleep. Continuously the idea haunted him—his spitting on the Buddha, one of the most insulting things, and Buddha remaining as calm and quiet as he had been before, as if nothing had happened, wiping his face and saying to him, "Thank you, sir. And whenever you have this desire to spit on somebody, please come to us."

He remembered it again and again. That face, that calm and quiet face, those compassionate eyes. And when he had said thank you, it had not been just a formality; he was really grateful. His whole being was saying that he was grateful; his whole atmosphere was grateful. Just as the man could see that Ananda was red-hot with anger, Buddha was so cool, so loving, so compassionate. He could not forgive himself now; what had he done? Spitting on that man—a man like Buddha!

Early the next morning he rushed back, fell down at the feet of Buddha, and said, "Forgive me, sir. I could not sleep the whole night."

Buddha said, "Forget all about it. There is no need to ask forgiveness for something which has already passed.

"So much water has gone down the Ganges." Buddha was sitting on the bank of the Ganges under a tree. He showed the man: "Look, each moment so much water is flowing down! Twenty-four hours have passed—why are you carrying it, something which is no longer existential? Forget all about it.

> There is no need to ask forgiveness for something which has already passed.

"And I cannot forgive you, because, in the first place, I was not angry with you. If I had been angry, I could have forgiven you. If you really need forgiveness, ask Ananda. Fall at his feet—he will enjoy it!"

To those who have helped, to those who have hindered, to those who have been indifferent—be grateful to all, because all together they are creating the context in which buddhas are born, in which you can become a buddha.

> What is meditation? Becoming aware of what you are doing, becoming aware of what is happening to you.

And remember, each situation has to become an opportunity to meditate.

What is meditation? Becoming aware of what you are doing, becoming aware of what is happening to you. Somebody insults you—become aware.

What is happening to you when the insult reaches you? Meditate over it; this is changing the whole gestalt. When somebody insults you, you concentrate on the person—"Why is he insulting me? Who does he think he is? How can I take revenge?" If he is very powerful, you surrender, you start wagging your tail. If he is not very powerful, and you see that he is weak, you pounce on him. But you forget yourself completely in all this; the other becomes the focus. This is missing an opportunity for meditation. When somebody insults you, meditate.

Gurdjieff has said, "When my father was dying, I was only nine. He called me close to his bed and whispered in my ear, 'My son, I am not leaving much to you, not in worldly things, but I have one thing to tell you that was told to me by my father on his deathbed. It has helped me tremendously; it has been my treasure. You are not very grown up yet, you may not understand what I am saying, but keep it, remember it. One day you will be grown up, and then you may understand. This is a key: it unlocks the doors of great treasures.'"

Of course Gurdjieff could not understand it at that moment, but it was the thing that changed his whole life. And his father said a very simple thing. He said, "Whenever somebody insults you, my son, tell him you will meditate over it for twenty-four hours and then you will come and answer him."

Gurdjieff could not believe that this was such a great key. He could not believe that this was something so valuable that he had to remember it. And we can forgive a young child of nine years old. But because this was something said by his dying father—who had loved him tremendously, and immediately after saying it, he breathed his last—it became imprinted on him; he could not forget it. Whenever he remembered his father, he would remember the saying.

Without truly understanding, he started practicing it. If somebody insulted him, he would say, "Sir, for twenty-four hours I have to meditate over it—that's what my father told me. And he is here no longer, and I cannot disobey an old dead man. He loved me tremendously, and I loved him tremendously, and now there is no way to disobey him. You can disobey your father when he is alive, but when your father is dead how can you disobey him? So please forgive me, I will come after twenty-four hours and answer you."

And he says, "Meditating on it for twenty-four hours has given me the greatest insights into my being. Sometimes I found that the insult was right, that that's how I am. So I would go to the person and say, 'Sir, thank you, you were right. It was not an insult, it was simply a statement of fact. You called me stupid; I am.'

"Or sometimes it happened that meditating for twenty-four hours, I would come to know that it was an absolute lie. But when something is a lie, why be offended by it? So I would not even go to tell him that it was a lie. A lie is a lie—why be bothered by it?"

But watching, meditating, slowly, slowly he became more and more aware of his reactions, rather than the actions of others.

Watch: whatsoever arises out of the ego, whatsoever is an ego trip, immediately disconnect yourself from it. Even to linger with it for a little while is dangerous because lingering will give it energy. The moment you know it is an ego trip, immediately disconnect yourself. And everybody knows when they are going on an ego trip. It is not an art to be learned; everybody is born with it. You know it! You can go with it in spite of your knowing, that is another matter—but you know it. Whenever pride arises, whenever the ego raises its head, you know it. Cut off that head immediately, in a single blow.

And whatever good happens to you, immediately share it. This is one of the most fundamental things. Don't hoard it; don't be a miser. If love has arisen, share it, shower it. If you cannot find people, shower it on the trees, on the rocks, but shower it. Don't hoard it—because if you hoard it, it turns into poison; if you hoard it, it goes sour and bitter. Share it. The more you share, the more will be coming into you from unknown sources. Slowly, slowly, you will be able to know the ways of inner economics.

The outer economics is: hoard if you want to have things. And the inner economics is just the opposite: hoard, and you will not have it. Give, and you will have it; give more, and you will have more of it.

3

No Longer Many, but One

The moment you drop the false values imposed upon you, resentment also will disappear.

And remember, when your resentment disappears, then for the first time you will be able to be loving toward your father, toward your mother, toward your brothers, sisters, toward your teachers—because you will have the understanding that whatsoever they did, there was no bad intention behind it. They were simply doing to you what was done to them by their teachers, by their parents. You will have a deep compassion for them. You will have a new feeling arising in you, of love—and of sadness too, because those people have missed.

The day you can feel sad that your father and your mother have missed life, do you think you will be still angry against them? You will feel great love. Just go once in a while and share your love, share your song, share your dance. They will be surprised, and you will be surprised also. They will be surprised that this boy who has always been a troublemaker in the family has become so peaceful, so serene, just a silent lake full of lotus flowers.

And you will be surprised that they are not treating you the way they used to treat you. In fact, you will see that they want to understand what has happened to you. You look so beautiful, you look a totally new being—what has happened? They would like to know, and they would desire, if it is possible, for them also to be in the same space you are in.

. . .

Parent—Adult—Child

Man is a crowd. A crowd of many voices—relevant, irrelevant, consistent, inconsistent, each voice pulling in its own way, all the voices pulling you apart. Ordinarily man is a mess, virtually a kind of madness. You somehow manage, you somehow manage to look sane. Deep down, layers and layers of insanity are boiling within you. They can erupt at any moment. Your control can be lost at any moment because your control is enforced from without. It is not a discipline that has come from your center of being.

For social reasons, economic reasons, political reasons, you have enforced a certain character upon yourself. But many vital forces exist against that character within you; they are continuously sabotaging your character. Hence, every day you go on committing many mistakes, many errors. Even sometimes you feel that you never wanted to do it; in spite of yourself, you go on committing many mistakes—because you are not one, you are many.

A man like Gautam Buddha does not call these mistakes "sins" because to call them sin will be condemning you. He simply calls them misdemeanors, mistakes, errors. To err is human; not to err is divine. And the way from the human to the divine goes through mindfulness. These many voices within you can stop torturing you, pulling you, push-ing you. These many voices can disappear, if you become mindful.

In a mindful state, mistakes are not committed—not that you con-trol them—but in a mindful state, in an alert, aware state, voices, the many voices, cease. You simply be-come one, and whatsoever you do

> Your child says one thing, your parent says something else, and your adult, rational mind says something else.

comes from the very core of your being. It is never wrong. This has to be understood.

In the language of the modern Humanistic Potential Move-ment, there is a parallel to understand it. It is what Transactional Analysis calls the triangle of "PAC." "P" means "parent"; "A" means "adult"; "C" means "child." These are your three layers, as if you are a three-storied building. The first floor is that of the child; the second floor is that of the parent; the third floor is that of the adult. All three exist together.

This is your inner triangle and conflict. Your child says one thing, your parent says something else, and your adult, rational mind says something else.

The Child Says "Enjoy"

For the child, this moment is the only moment; he has no other considerations. The child is spontaneous, but unaware of the consequences—unaware of past, unaware of future. He lives in the moment. He has no values, and he has no mindfulness, no awareness. The child consists of felt concepts; he lives through feeling. His whole being is irrational.

Of course, he comes into many conflicts with others. He comes into many contradictions within himself because one feeling helps him to do one thing, then suddenly he starts feeling another feeling. A child can never complete anything. By the time he can complete it, his feeling has changed. He starts many things but never comes to any conclusion. A child remains inconclusive.

The child enjoys—but the enjoyment is not creative, cannot be creative. The child delights—but life cannot be lived only through delight. You cannot remain a child forever. You will have to learn many things because you are not alone here. If you were alone, then there would be no question—you could have remained a child forever! But the society is there; millions of people are there. You have to follow many rules, you have to follow many values—otherwise, there will be so much conflict that life would become impossible. The child has to be disciplined—and that's where the parent comes in.

Parental Controls

The parental voice in you is the voice of the society, culture, civilization, the voice that makes you capable of living in a world where you are not alone—where there are many individuals with conflicting ambitions, where there is much struggle for survival, where there is much conflict. You have to pave your path, and you have to move very cautiously. The parental voice is that of caution. It makes you civilized. The child is wild; the parental voice helps you to become civilized. The word *civil* is good. It means one who has become capable of living in a city, who has become capable of being a member of a group, of a society.

The child is very dictatorial—the child thinks he is the center of the world. The parent has to teach you that you are not the center of the world, that everybody thinks that way, but the parent has to make you more and more alert that there are many people in the world, you are not alone. You have to consider them if you want yourself to be considered by them. Otherwise, you will be crushed. It is a sheer question of survival, of policy, of politics. The parental voice gives you commandments—what to do, what not to do. The "feeling" simply goes through life blind—the parent makes you cautious. It is needed.

And then there is the third voice within you, the third layer, when you have become adult and you are no longer controlled by your parents. Your own reason has come of age; you can think on your own.

The child consists of *felt* concepts, the parent consists of *taught* concepts, and the adult consists of *thought* concepts. And these three layers are continuously fighting. The child says one thing, the parent says just the opposite, and the adult reason may say something totally different.

You see beautiful food—the child says to eat as much as you want. The parental voice says that many things have to be considered—whether you are really feeling hungry, or just the smell of the food, the taste of the food is the only appeal. Is this food really nutritious? Is it going to nourish your body, or can it become harmful to you? Wait, listen, don't rush. And then there is the rational mind, the adult mind, which may say something totally different.

There is no necessity that your adult mind agrees with your parents. Your parents were not omniscient; they were not all-knowing. They were as much fallible human beings as you are, and many times you find loopholes in their thinking. Many times you find them very dogmatic, superstitious, believing in foolish things, irrational ideologies. Your adult says no; your parent says do it. Your adult says it is not worth doing, and your child goes on pulling you somewhere else. This is the triangle within you.

The Triangle Within You

If you listen to the child, your parent feels angry. So one part feels good—you can go on eating as much ice cream as you want—but your parent inside feels angry. A part of you starts condemning, and then you start feeling guilty. The same guilt arises as it used to arise when you were really a child. You are no longer a child—but the child has not disappeared. It is there; it is just your ground floor, your very base, your foundation. If you follow the child, if you follow the feeling, the parent is angry, and then you start feeling guilt. If you follow the parent, then your child feels that he is being forced into things he does not want to do. Then your child feels he is being unnecessarily interfered with, unnecessarily trespassed upon. Freedom is lost when you listen to the parent and your child starts feeling rebellious.

If you listen to the parent, your adult mind says, "What nonsense! These people never knew anything." You know more; you are more in tune with the modern world; you are more contemporary. These ideologies are just dead ideologies, out of date— why are you bothering? If you listen to your reason, then you also feel as if you are betraying your parents. Again, guilt arises.

What to do? And it is almost impossible to find something on which all these three layers agree. This is human anxiety. No, never do all these three layers agree on any point. There is no agreement ever.

Now, there are teachers who believe in the child. They emphasize the child more. For example, Lao Tzu. He says, "The agreement is not going to come. You drop this parental voice, these commandments, these Old Testaments. Drop all 'shoulds' and become a child again." That's also what Jesus says. Lao Tzu and Jesus, their emphasis is: become a child again because only with the child will you be able to gain your spontaneity, will you again become part of the natural flow, Tao.

Their message is beautiful but seems to be almost impractical. Sometimes, yes, it has happened—a person has become a child again. But it is so exceptional that it is not possible to think that humanity is ever going to become a child again. It is beautiful like a star: far, distant, but out of reach.

Then there are other teachers—Mahavira, Moses, Mohammed, Manu—they say listen to the parental voice, listen to the moral, what the society says, what you have been taught. Listen and follow it. If you want to be at ease in the world, if you want to be peaceful in the world, listen to the parent. Never go against the parental voice. That's what the world has followed, more or less. But then, one never feels spontaneous, one never feels natural. One always feels confined, caged. And when you don't feel free, you may feel peaceful, but that peacefulness is worthless. Unless peace comes with freedom, you cannot accept it. Unless peace comes with bliss, you cannot accept it. It brings convenience, comfort, but your soul suffers.

Yes, there have been a few people again who have achieved through the parental voice, who have really attained to the truth. But that too is very rare. And that world is gone. Maybe in the past, Moses and Manu and Mohammed were useful. They gave commandments to the world: "Do this, don't do that." They made things simple, very simple. They have not left anything for you to decide; they don't trust that you will be able to decide. They simply give you a ready-made formula: "These are the ten commandments to be followed. You simply do these, and all that you hope, all that you desire will happen as a consequence. You just be obedient."

All the old religions emphasized obedience too much. "Disobedience is the only sin"—that's what Christianity says. "Adam and Eve were expelled from the Garden of Eden because they disobeyed. God had said not to eat the fruit of the tree of knowledge, and they disobeyed." That was their only sin. But every child is committing that sin! The father says, "Don't smoke," and the child tries it. The father says, "Don't go to the movie," and he goes. The story of Adam and Eve is the story of every child. And then condemnation, expulsion . . .

Obedience is religion for Manu, Mohammed, Moses. But that world has gone, and through it many have not attained. Many became peaceful, good citizens—good members, respectable members of the society—but nothing much more than that.

Then there is the third emphasis on being adult. Confucius, Patanjali, or modern agnostics—Bertrand Russell, all humanists of the world—they all emphasize: "Believe only in your own reason." That seems very arduous, so much so that one's whole life becomes just a conflict, because you have been brought up by your parents, you have been conditioned by your parents. If you listen only to your reason, you have to deny many things in your being. In fact, your whole mind has to be denied. It is not easy to erase it. Also, as children you were born without any reason. That too is there.

Basically, you are a feeling being; reason comes very late. It comes when, in fact, all that has to happen has happened. Psychologists say a child learns almost seventy-five percent of his entire knowledge by the time he is seven years old. Seventy-five percent of his entire knowledge he has learned by the time he is seven years old, fifty percent by the time he is four years old. All this learning happens when you are a child, and reason is a very late arrival.

It is very difficult to live by reason. People have tried—a Bertrand Russell here and there—but nobody has achieved truth through it, because reason alone is not enough. All these angles have been chosen and tried, and nothing has worked.

Move in the Very Center

Buddha's standpoint is totally different—that's his original contribution to human consciousness. He says not to choose any. He says, move in the center of the triangle. Don't choose reason, don't choose the parent, don't choose the child—just move in the very center of the triangle and remain silent and become mindful—his approach is tremendously meaningful—and then you will be able to have a clear perspective of your being. And out of that perspective and clarity, let the response come.

We can say it in another way: if you function as a child, that is a childish reaction. Many times you function as a child. Somebody says something and you get hurt—and a tantrum and anger and temper, you lose everything. Later on you feel very bad about it—you lost your image: everybody thinks you are so sober, and you were so childish. And nothing much was even at stake! Or you follow your parental voice, but later on you think that still you are dominated by your parents. You have not yet become an adult, mature enough to take the reins of your life into your own hands. Or sometimes you follow reason, but then you think that reason is not enough, feeling also is needed. And without feeling, a rational being becomes just a head; he loses contact with the body, he loses contact with life, he becomes disconnected. He functions only as a thinking mechanism. But thinking cannot make you alive; in thinking there is no juice of life. It is a very dry thing. Then you hanker, you hanker for something that can again allow your energies to flow, that can again allow you to be green and alive and young.

This goes on, and you go on chasing your own tail.

Buddha says these are all reactions, and any reaction is bound to be partial. Only *response* is total, and whatsoever is partial is a mistake. That's Buddha's definition of error: whatsoever is partial is a mistake because your other parts will remain unfulfilled and they will take their revenge. Be total. Response is total; reaction is partial.

When you listen to one voice and follow it, you are getting into trouble. You will never be satisfied with it. Only one part will be satisfied; the other two parts will be very much dissatisfied. So two-thirds of your being will be dissatisfied, one-third of your being will be satisfied, and you will always remain in a turmoil. Whatsoever you do, *reaction* can never satisfy you because reaction is partial.

Response—*response* is total. Then you don't function from any triangle. You don't choose; you simply remain in a choiceless awareness. You remain centered. And out of that centering, you act, whatsoever it is. It is neither child nor parent nor adult. You have gone beyond "PAC." It is *you* now—neither the child nor the parent nor the adult. It is you, your being. That PAC is like a cyclone, and your center is the center of the cyclone.

So whenever there is a need to respond, the first thing, Buddha says, is become mindful. Become aware. Remember your center. Become grounded in your center. Be there for a few moments before you do anything. There is no need to think about it, because thinking is partial. There is no need to feel about it, because feeling is partial. There is no need to find clues from your parents, Bible, Koran, Gita—these are all "P"—there is no need. You simply remain tranquil, silent. Simply alert: watching the situation as if you are absolutely out of it, aloof, a watcher on the hills.

This is the first requirement: to be centered whenever you want to act. Then out of this centering, let the act arise—and whatsoever you do will be virtuous, whatsoever you do will be right.

Looking Back, Looking In

Repentance means retrospective awareness; repentance means looking backward.

You have done something. If you were aware, then no wrong could have happened, but you were not aware at the time you did it. Somebody insulted you; you became angry, you hit him on the head. You were not aware of what you were doing. Now things have cooled down; the situation has gone; you are no longer angry; you can look backward more easily. You missed awareness at that time.

The best thing was to have awareness at that time, but you missed it, and now there is no point in crying and weeping over

> Repentance means retrospective awareness; repentance means looking backward.

spilled milk. But you can look, you can bring awareness to that which has already happened.

That is what Mahavira calls *pratikraman*: looking back—what Patanjali calls *pratyahar*: looking in. That's what Jesus calls *repentance*. That's what Buddha calls *paschatap*. It is not feeling sorry, it is not just feeling bad about it—because that is not going to help. It is becoming aware. It is reliving the experience as it should have been. You have to move into it again.

You missed awareness in that moment; you were overwhelmed by unconsciousness. Now things have cooled, you can take your awareness, the light of awareness, back. You move into that incident again; you look into it again as you should have really done. It is gone, but you can do it retrospectively in your mind. This looking back, continuously looking back, will make you more and more aware.

There are three stages. You have done something, then you become aware—first stage. Second stage: you are doing something, and you become aware. And third stage: you are going to do something, and you become aware. Only in the third stage will your life be transformed. But the first two are necessary for the third; they are necessary steps.

Whenever you can become aware, become aware. You have been angry—now sit down, meditate, become aware what has happened. Ordinarily we do it, but we do for the wrong reasons. We do it to put our image back in its right place. You always think you are a very loving person, compassionate, and then you suddenly become angry. Now your image is distorted in your own eyes. You do a sort of repentance. You go to the person, and you say, "I am sorry."

> Real repentance is remembering it, going into the details fully aware of what happened, going backward, reliving the experience. Reliving the experience is like unwinding; it erases.

What are you doing? You are repainting your image. Your ego is trying to repaint the image because you have fallen in your own eyes, you have fallen in others' eyes. Now you are trying to rationalize.

At least you can go and say, "I am sorry. I did it in spite of myself. I don't know how it happened, I don't know what evil force took possession of me, but I am sorry. Forgive me." You are trying to come back to the same level where you were before you became angry.

This is a trick of the ego; this is not real repentance. Again you will do the same thing.

Real repentance is remembering it, going into the details fully aware of what happened, going backward, reliving the experience. Reliving the experience is like unwinding; it erases.

And not only that—it makes you capable of more awareness, because awareness is practiced when you are remembering it, when you are again becoming aware about the past incident. You are getting a discipline in awareness, in mindfulness. Next time, you will become aware a little earlier.

This time you were angry; after two hours you could cool down. Next time after one hour you will cool down. Next time after a few minutes. Next time, just as it has happened you will cool down and you will be able to see. By and by, by slow progression, one day while you are angry you will catch hold of yourself red-handed. And that is a beautiful experience—to catch yourself red-handed committing an error. Then suddenly the whole quality changes because whenever awareness penetrates you, reactions stop.

This anger is a childish reaction, it is the child in you. It is coming from the "C." And later on, when you feel sorry, that is coming from the "P," from the parent. The parent forces you to feel sorry and go and ask forgiveness. You have not been good to your mother or to your uncle—go and put things right.

Or it can come from "A," from your adult mind. You have been angry, and later on you recognize that this is going to be too much; there is a financial loss in it. You have been angry with your boss, now you become afraid. Now you start thinking he may throw you out, or he may carry the anger within him. Your salary was going to be raised; he may not raise it—a thousand and one things—you would like to put things right.

When a buddha says repent, he's not telling you to function from C or P or A. He is saying, when you become aware, sit down, close your eyes, meditate upon the whole thing—become a watcher. You missed the situation, but still something can be done about it: you can watch it. You can watch it as it should have been watched. You can practice; this will be a rehearsal, and by the time you have watched the whole situation, you will feel completely okay.

If then you feel like going and asking forgiveness, for no other reasons—neither the parent, nor the adult, nor the child—but out of sheer understanding, out of sheer meditation that it was wrong . . . It was not wrong for any other reason; it was wrong because you behaved in an unconscious way.

Let me repeat it:

Go and ask for forgiveness—not for any other reason: financial, social, political, cultural—you simply go there because you meditated on it, and you recognized and you realized the fact that you acted in unawareness; you have hurt somebody in unawareness.

You have to go and console the person at least. You have to go and help the person to understand your helplessness—that you are an unconscious person, that you are a human being with all the limitations, that you are sorry. It is not putting your ego back; it is simply doing something that your meditation has showed you. It is totally a different dimension.

Ordinarily what do we do? We become defensive. If you have been angry at your wife or at your child, you become defensive;

you say it had to be done that way, it was needed. It was needed for the child's own good. If you are not angry, how are you going to discipline the child? If you are not angry with somebody, people will take advantage of you. You are not a coward; you are a brave man. How can you just let people do things that should not be done to you? You have to react.

You become defensive; you rationalize. If you go on rationalizing your errors . . . And all errors can be rationalized, remember it. There exists not a single error which cannot be rationalized. You can rationalize everything. But then, such a person is bound to become more and more unconscious, more and more deeply unaware. If you go on defending yourself, you will not be able to transform yourself. You have to recognize that there is something wrong. The very recognition helps change.

Ordinarily, even if we sometimes recognize that, "Yes, something wrong has happened," we don't try to reform ourselves; we only try to reform our image. We want to feel that everybody has forgiven us. We want everybody to recognize that it was wrong on our part, but we have asked for their forgiveness, and things are put right again. We are again on our pedestal. The fallen image is placed back on the throne. We don't reform ourselves.

> If you go on defending yourself, you will not be able to transform yourself. You have to recognize that there is something wrong. The very recognition helps change.

> If you have really asked forgiveness, then it should not happen again. Only that can be a proof that you are really on the path of changing yourself.

You have asked forgiveness many times, but again and again you go on doing the same thing. That simply shows that it was a policy, politics, a trick to manipulate people—but you have remained the same, you have not changed at all. If you have really asked forgiveness for your anger, or any offense against anybody, then it should not happen again. Only that can be a proof that you are really on the path of changing yourself.

Watch how many things you do unconsciously. Somebody says something, and there is anger. There is not even a single moment's gap. It is as if you are just a mechanism—somebody pushes a button, and you lose your temper. Just as if you push the button, and the fan starts moving and the light goes on. There is not a single moment. The fan never thinks whether to move or not to move; it simply moves.

This is unconsciousness; this is mindlessness. Somebody insults, and you are simply controlled by his insult. But if you are conscious enough that you can wait for twenty-four seconds before you react, then it is finished! Then you cannot be angry. Then you have missed the moment to be angry, then you have missed the train; the train has left the platform. Even twenty-four seconds will do—you try it.

So don't miss any opportunity, whenever you can become aware. And those are the best moments—when unconsciousness pulls you deep down. If you can use those moments, if you can use those moments as challenges, existence will become more and more aware in you. One day your awareness becomes a continuous flame, an eternal flame. Then existence is perfectly awake: no sleep, no dream.

This is the meaning of the word *buddha*. *Buddha* means "one who has become absolutely aware." In no situation does he lose his mindfulness. His mindfulness has become just natural like breathing. Just as you breathe in and breathe out, in exactly the same way a buddha inhales awareness, exhales awareness. His centering has become permanent. He does not function from personalities— the personality of the child, the parent, the adult—no. He simply functions from a point that is beyond all personalities.

Let me repeat one thing so that you can remember it.

You have three layers: the child, the parent, the adult—and you are none of them.

You are neither the child nor the parent nor the adult. You are something beyond; you are something eternal; you are something far away from all these struggling parts, conflicting parts.

Don't choose; just be mindful and act out of your mindfulness. Then you will be spontaneous like a child and without being childish. And remember the difference between being like a child and being childish. They are two different things.

If you act out of mindfulness, you will be like a child, and yet you will not be childish. And if you act out of your mindfulness, you will be following all the commandments without following them at all. And if you act out of your mindfulness, whatsoever you do will be reasonable. And to be reasonable is to be really rational.

And remember, reasonableness is different from rationality. Reasonableness is a very different thing because reasonableness accepts irrationality also as part of life. Reason is monotonous; rationality is monotonous. Reasonableness accepts the polarity of things. A reasonable person is a feeling person as much as a reasoning person.

So if you act out of your innermost core, you will become tremendously content; contented because all layers will be fulfilled. Your child will be fulfilled because you will be spontaneous. Your parent will not feel angry and guilty, because all that is good will be done by you naturally, not as an outer discipline but as an inner awareness.

You will follow the Ten Commandments of Moses without ever having heard about them; you will naturally follow them. That's where Moses got them—not on the mountain but on the inner peak. You will be following Lao Tzu and Jesus—and you may not have even heard about Lao Tzu and Jesus. That's where they got their childhood again; that's where they were born. And you will be following Manu and Mahavira and Mohammed, very naturally, and still you will not be irrational. Your mind will be in total support with it. It will not be against your adult rationality. Your adult rationality will be totally convinced by it, your Bertrand Russell will be convinced by it.

Then all your three conflicting parts fall into one whole. You become a unity; you are together. Then those many voices disappear. Then you are no longer many, you are one. This one is the goal.

4

The Tao of Letting Go

ave you watched one thing? It is very difficult to deceive a small child. Even very cunning people find it very difficult. If a small child is carrying a hundred-dollar bill, nobody will be able to cheat the child. It will be very difficult to cheat the child. Why?—because of the trust, the innocence, the very innocence. And if you take the money from the child, you will never be able to forgive yourself. That memory will haunt you forever and ever; it will create hell for you.

Have you watched? You are sitting on a railway platform, and you ask some stranger who is sitting by your side, "Please, just take a little care of my luggage; I am going to purchase a ticket." You are leaving your suitcases, all your things in the hands of an unknown stranger. Who knows? He may escape with the whole thing, but it never happens. Why does it never happen? Because of trust. How can that person deceive you? You trusted him, an unknown stranger. If *you* are watching your luggage, he may steal something, that is possible—but if you leave your luggage to him and go to purchase a ticket, it is impossible. What makes it impossible?

Trust has its own power. Trust has its own energy, its own vibe. The very gesture, that you trusted, makes it impossible; the person cannot deceive you.

That means, when people deceive you, it is not only their fault. You are also at fault. You must be carrying mistrust in you, and they got the vibe. If trust prevents them from deceiving you, then your mistrust about people must be creating an atmosphere in which deceiving becomes easier for them.

. . .

The Man Who Lost His Memory

A story:

In middle age, Hua-tʒu of Yang-li in Sung lost his memory. He would receive a present in the morning and forget it by the evening; give a present in the evening and forget it by the morning. In the street, he would forget to walk; at home he would forget to sit down. Today he would not remember yesterday; tomorrow he would not remember today. His family were troubled about it and invited a diviner to tell his fortune but without success. They invited a shaman to perform an auspicious rite, but it made no difference. They invited a doctor to treat him, but it did no good.

There was a Confucian of Lu who, acting as his own go-between, claimed that he could cure it. Hua-tzu's wife and children offered half of their property in return for his skill.

The Confucian told them: "This is clearly not a disease which can be divined by hexagrams and omens, or charmed away by auspicious prayers, or treated by medicines and the needle. I shall try reforming his mind, changing his thoughts; there is a good chance that he will recover."

Then the Confucian tried stripping Hua-tzu, and Hua-tzu looked for his clothes; tried starving him, and he looked for food; tried shutting him up in the dark, and he looked for light. The Confucian was delighted, and told the man's sons:

"The sickness is curable, but my arts have been passed down secretly through the generations and are not disclosed to outsiders. I shall shut out his attendants and stay alone with him in his room for seven days."

The sons agreed, and no one knew what methods the Confucian used, but the sickness of many years was completely dispelled in a single morning.

When Hua-tzu woke up, he was very angry. He dismissed his wife, punished his sons, and chased away the Confucian with a spear. The authorities of Sung arrested him and wanted to know the reason for his behavior.

"Formerly, when I forgot," said Hua-tzu, "I was boundless; I did not notice whether heaven and earth existed or not. Now suddenly I remember, and all the disasters and recoveries, gains and losses, joys and sorrows, loves and hates *of twenty or thirty years past rise up in a thousand tangled threads. I fear that all the disasters and recoveries, gains and losses, joys and sorrows, loves and hates still to come will confound my heart just as much. Shall I never again find a moment of forgetfulness?"*

This is one of the greatest parables of Lieh Tzu, pregnant with profound significance and insight. Based on a great experience of the inner world of consciousness, it is paradoxical, but it indicates something absolute. Let us go into it very softly, delicately, carefully. It has much to give you; it has much to show to you. It can give great clarity to you on your path.

Before we enter into it, a few paradigms of Taoism will be helpful.

First, Taoism believes that memory is the problem. Because of memory, we are not really alive.

Memory holds us back in the past; it never allows us to be in the present. It is a dead weight. It goes on growing every day. Every day the past becomes bigger and bigger and bigger. Every day more and more experiences, more and more memories become accumulated. And they hold you back.

> Memory holds us back in the past; it never allows us to be in the present.

The child is free. He has no past. The old man is not free. He has a long past. The child has nothing to look back to; he has everything to look forward to—he has the future just opening up for him, a great adventure. The old man has nothing in the future. Everything has happened, and all that has happened goes on cluttering his mind. It is a weight that pulls him down, backward; it does not allow him to go with the times. He lags behind.

Memory is how you are rooted in the past. Unless you become so free of memory that you need not look back—memory no longer disturbs you; memory no longer clouds you—you will not be able to live in the present. If you cannot live in the present, the future is not yours—because the future is contacted only through living in the present. The future becomes a reality only through living in the present.

The present is the door by which the future enters and the past goes out. If you are looking at the past, you will miss the future because during the time you are looking at the past, the future is entering into the present, and you cannot look both ways simultaneously. You have eyes to look forward; you don't have eyes at the back of your head. Nature never intended you to look back; otherwise, your eyes would have been at the back of your head. Nature has intended that you should look forward; nature has not given you any instrument to look backward.

When you look back, you have to turn around, and during the moment you are looking back, and your head is turned to the dead past, the future is turning into the present. You will miss that birth; you will always miss the future turning into the present—which is the only reality there is.

Now, what happens? If you are too interested in the past, too attached to your memories, you start creating an unreal future in the imagination. A man who is too attached to the past projects his future also. He lives in his memory, and through his memory he creates an imagined future. Both are unreal.

The past is no more; you cannot live it again—there is no possibility of that. That which is gone is gone forever; it is impossible to bring it back. Because it is impossible to bring it back, you start imagining a similar type of future, something similar—a little more decorated, a little sweeter, a little better. You start imagining a future, but that future is based on your past experience. What else can it be based on?

You loved a woman. Almost everything was good in the woman except for a few things. Now you project a dream: in the future you will find a woman who will be as good as the past woman but with those wrong habits deleted, with those wrong habits dropped. In the future you will have a house as beautiful as in the past, even more beautiful, but with a few things that were not there in the past. You will manage the future.

Your imagination is nothing but a modified past. This is how people are living. The past is no more, and the future is nothing but a desire to repeat the past—of course in a better way, but it is the same past. You ate something yesterday; you would like to eat it again tomorrow. Yesterday you loved a man or a woman; tomorrow you would like to love a man or a woman again. You want to repeat your past. The mind is a repetitive mechanism; the mind continuously hankers for sameness.

Reality is new every moment; it is never the same. You cannot step into the same river twice; life is constantly moving, changing. Only change is permanent; everything else is changing. Only change is not changing—that is reality—but then you create a false, pseudo-reality of your own invention, fabricated in the mind, manufactured by your desire, and you start living in that.

Taoism says that to be in reality, one has to come out of the mind; one must become a no-mind. To be in reality, one has to uproot oneself from the past. One has to forget the past. To remember that which is, the eyes have to be completely unclouded from the past—only then can you see in reality. Eyes clouded with the past are blind eyes.

You are not really blind, you are just clouded by your past. You cannot see directly because of so many screens covering your eyes. Those screens have been created by your past.

A man insulted you yesterday, and today you come across him on the road. The past arises, a screen falls over your eyes: this is the same man who insulted you! You have to take revenge; you have to pay him back in the same coin, tit for tat.

You start getting angry; you get into a rage. Now you are missing this man. It is possible that this man is no longer the same—in fact, he cannot be the same. He may have repented; he may have brooded the whole night; he may have decided to come to you and apologize. He may be coming to apologize now, but you cannot see him: your eyes are clouded with anger, and your anger will color your reality.

Now, even if he tries to apologize, you will think that he must be trying to deceive you, or he has become afraid of your vengeance, or he is a very cunning man—beware, he is trying to cheat you, deceive you. Right now he is trying to befriend you, but some day he will again bring some trouble to you—all these thoughts will be there, and you will not be able to see what he is. You will miss the reality.

And, seeing all these clouds on your face, there is every possibility that although he had come to apologize, he may not apologize now! Seeing that you are in a rage, and you will not understand, he may change his own ideas—because we affect each other—and if he changes, your ideas are confirmed; they become even stronger. This is how things happen.

One who has clarity never carries the past. One simply looks into reality with no interference from the past. That is the meaning of this story.

No Mind of Your Own

Dropping memory means dropping the mind. Dropping the mind means dropping the whole world. Dropping the mind means dropping the ego—then you are no longer self-centered, then you don't have any mind whatsoever. Then you live a life with no mind of your own—that is the meaning of Tao. Then God's mind functions through you; you don't have your own mind. You function, but now you don't function from your own center. Now the center of the whole becomes your center. You act, but you are not the doer anymore; God acts. Your surrender is total.

Just the other day I was reading a beautiful Hassidic parable:

A young man asked an old rabbi, "In the past, in the old, golden days, we have heard that people used to see God with their own eyes. People used to encounter God. God used to walk on earth; God used to call people by their name. God was very close. What has happened now? Why is God not so close? Why can we not see him directly? Why is he hiding? Where has he gone? Why has he forgotten the earth? Why does he no longer walk on the earth? Why does he not hold the hands of people stumbling in darkness? He used to do that before."

The old rabbi looked at the disciple and said, "My son, he is still there where he used to be, but man has forgotten how to stoop down so low that he can see him."

To stoop down . . . Man has forgotten—man is standing very haughty; man is standing very proud; man is standing very erect. Man is standing separate from God. Man has become an island; man is no longer part of the universal, part of the whole—that's why. God is exactly where he used to be. He is still trying to hold your hand, but you are not willing. He is still confronting you, but you look sideways. He is still there, calling you by your own name, but you are full of your own noise—the inner talk, the continuous chattering; you have become a chatterbox—that's why.

Man has forgotten how to stoop, how to bow down.

In the East, bowing down has always been a very significant

gesture. The disciple goes to the master, bows down, lies down flat on the earth. That is a gesture of surrender. He says, "I am no more." He says, "I will not exist anymore as myself. Now I will be a vehicle; I will be passive. You pour, and I will be a womb; you pour and I will be a receptacle. I will not fight. I surrender." In that surrender, something of tremendous value happens: with the master, you start learning the ABC of surrender. Then one day, when you have learned what surrender is, you try it with the whole of existence.

The master is just a kindergarten, just a beginning, the beginning of surrender, of trust in existence. When you have learned the joy of it, the beauty of it, the benediction of it, then you want to go on to deeper seas. You have learned swimming near the banks; now you would like to go to the farthest point. Then godliness is available. But if you exist as *you*, if you exist as a self, then it is impossible. Then you exist as an ego.

Memory in this parable means ego. These Taoist parables are very subtle.

Now let us go into it.

In middle age, Hua-tzu of Yang-li in Sung lost his memory.

That is a way of saying that he became a meditator. That is a Taoist expression: "lost his memory." It means he became a nonindividual. It means he became a nonego. It means he became loose from the grip of the mind, dropped the weight of the past. It is not something condemnatory, remember; it is a great appreciation.

In Taoist circles, when somebody says, "Somebody has lost his memory," remember that he is praising the person. Taoists have their own way of saying things, very peculiar ways of saying things. But the meaning of their gestures is profound.

In middle age, Hua-tzu of Yang-li in Sung lost his memory. He became a no-mind, forgot all about his past, forgot all that had happened—as if all the dust on the mirror dropped away. He came to exist in the present—that's what it means.

He was no longer in the past; he did not exist through the past; he did not function through the past. He had started functioning in the immediate present. He now lived moment to moment—not gathering, not accumulating, not hoarding any knowledge or any information. Whatsoever the totality brought in the moment was all. If he felt hungry, he looked for food, but he had no idea about any food that he had eaten before. And the moment his appetite was fulfilled, he forgot all about it. He did not carry the idea in his mind; he had no fantasy about food, either before or after. The moment was all; the now and the here was all; there was no then, and there was no there.

This is the first *satori*—when one becomes loosened from the grip of the past, the hold of the past, as if a snake had slipped from its old skin. One has become absolutely new, like a tree which, dropping all the old leaves during the fall, has sprouted new leaves. The moment something becomes old, it is dropped immediately. One goes on slipping again and again into the present. It is a totally new style of life.

Look for it in your own life. How do you live? Do you bring in the past again and again? Do you always live through the past? Is your life too colored by memory? Then you are living the worldly life. To live in memory is to live in the world, *samsara*. To live without memory is to live in godliness; to live without memory is to live in nirvana, enlightenment.

Remember, by saying that Hua-tzu lost his memory, you should not translate it to mean that he became absentminded. No! That is not the meaning of it. To become absentminded is a totally different thing. It is a disease: memory persists but becomes distorted. You know, but you don't know clearly.

Absentmindedness

An absentminded person is not a person of Tao. An absentminded person is simply absentminded. The man of Tao is very much present; he is not absentminded. In fact, he is so present that his memory cannot interfere. His presence is tremendous; his presence is so intense, the light of presence is so intense, that his memory cannot interfere. He functions out of the present—you function out of memory.

When somebody becomes absentminded he looks as if he were ill, naturally, because he goes on forgetting. Not that he has really forgotten, but he remembers that he has forgotten—the difference must be understood. He remembers that he has forgotten; he knows that he knows, and yet he cannot remember it. That is the man who is absentminded.

I have heard many stories about Thomas Alva Edison. He was a man who could be called perfectly absentminded . . .

One day he went into a restaurant, ate his lunch, came out, and met a friend at the door on the street. They talked for a few minutes, and then the friend said, "Why don't you come with me and have your lunch?"

So Edison said, "Right! You have reminded me, I came for my lunch."

Then they went inside the same restaurant. The food was served. The friend said to Edison, "You look a little puzzled."

Edison said, "What's the matter? I don't feel any appetite at all."

And the waiter laughed, and he said, "Sir, you ate your lunch here just five minutes ago."

This is absentmindedness.

Once it happened that he forgot his own name. He was standing in a queue, and when his turn came and his name was called, he started looking here and there, looking for the man whose name had been called. And then somebody who was standing behind him said to him, "Sir, as far as I know, you are Edison; who are you looking for?"

And Edison said, "Thank you. In fact, I had completely forgotten."

This is absentmindedness. Edison was not a man of *satori*; he still lived in his memory, but his memory was a chaos. He could not figure out what was what. He was not a Buddha; he was not a Hua-tzu. He did not live in the moment; he still lived in the past. Of course, his past was very clumsy. Absentmindedness is a clumsy past, a clumsy memory, a lousy memory.

Presence of Mind

But a man who has lost his memory, in the sense that Taoists use this term, is a man who functions out of the presence of his mind—presence of mind.

Just a few days ago I was reading the memoirs of a very rare man. He was a saint who died a few years ago. He lived for a really long time—almost one hundred and forty years. His name was Shivapuri Baba, Shivapuri Baba of Nepal. In his memoirs he tells a story:

He went to Jaipur, and a very rich man gave him a box full of money, one-hundred-rupee notes. While in the train he looked into the box; it was full of rupees, and he wanted to know how many he had. He started counting. In the compartment there were only two persons: Shivapuri Baba, himself a very old ancient man—at the time he must have been about one hundred and twenty years old—and an English lady, a young woman. She became interested. This old beggar was in the first class compartment and was carrying a whole box of one-hundred-rupee notes.

She suddenly had an idea. She jumped up and said, "Give me half the money; otherwise, I will pull the chain, and I will tell them that you tried to rape me."

Shivapuri Baba laughed and put his hands to his ears as if he were deaf. And he gave her some paper and said, "Write it down. I cannot hear." So she wrote it down. He took it and put it in his pocket and said, "Now pull the chain."

This is presence of mind! It is not functioning out of the past, because this has never happened before, and it may not happen again. But in a flash, like lightning, a man who is really present will act out of his presence.

You would have been in trouble because you would have looked into your memory—what should I do now? You would have started groping in your memory: Is there something in the past from which I can have some idea of what to do now?

In real life, nothing is ever repeated. Everything is new. That's why your responses always fall short. You act out of the past, and this thing is absolutely new—it has never happened before, so in fact you don't have any experience of it. Your experience may be of something similar, but it cannot be about exactly the same thing; it is not a repetition. The situation never repeats—maybe it was something similar: you were cheated by somebody; you were deceived by somebody; you were threatened by somebody—something similar, but not exactly the same. So when you start looking into your memory, you are showing that you don't have presence of mind.

This looks like a paradox: a man of no-mind is a man with presence of mind. And a man of mind, a man with memory, is a man who is absent. He looks into the past.

The situation is herenow, confronting you; it is an encounter. Re-

> In real life, nothing is ever repeated. Everything is new. That's why your responses always fall short.

spond right now, like a mirror. A mirror reflects whosoever comes in front of it. It does not look into memory: "this man has been here before, in front of me, so how to reflect him?" It simply reflects.

When there is no memory, it is not absentmindedness. The mirror is simply clear: the dust is not there; the dust is not a distraction. The reflection will be clear, and out of that reflection will come the act. When you act out of the present moment, your act is always total. You will never feel frustrated.

This story of Hua-tzu is about a man who lost his memory, who lost his mind, who lost his past—who became unburdened. To say it in Christ's words: he is one who became a child again, capable of entering into the kingdom of God.

But to his family, to his friends, he must have posed a great problem—naturally. They must have wondered what had happened to this old man—a calamity! They must have thought that he had fallen into a deep sleep, a sort of sleep. But exactly the contrary was the case—they were asleep, and this man had awakened from sleep. But they could understand only the language of sleep, so they must have thought that he had fallen asleep.

Becoming a Child Again

A big-city hustler made a wrong turn and found himself helplessly lost in the sticks of Kentucky. After bouncing along a rocky country road for more than an hour, he reached a large intersection. There, standing on the side of the road, was an old-looking mountain man.

"Hey, fellow!" he shouted. "Could you tell me where the road on the right leads to?"

"I don't rightly know," the old man answered slowly.

"Well, then, I wonder if you can tell me where the road on the left would take me?"

But again the old man shook his head. "I don't rightly know that either."

A little perturbed, the city fellow barked, "You're not too bright, are you?"

"Maybe not," drawled the mountain man, "but I ain't lost."

This old man, Hua-tzu, must have been thought by others to be lost. He had changed so tremendously that the whole village—his friends, his family, his sons, his daughters, his wife—must have become very worried. What should they do with this man?

He would receive a present in the morning and forget it by the evening . . .

He had really become a child again. That is the quality of innocence.

. . . give a present in the evening and forget it by the morning. In the street he would forget to walk; at home he would forget to sit down. Today he would not remember yesterday; tomorrow he would not remember today.

This is not absentmindedness. He was simply no longer gathering the past. It is not that he had a lousy memory; he was cut away from his memory utterly. He was like a child.

You are angry with a child, and the child is angry with you. Look at his face! He is so angry and so red that he would like to kill you. He says, "I will never talk to you again. Finished!" And the next moment he is sitting in your lap again and talking beautifully. He has forgotten. Whatsoever he has said in a rage, he has not carried it. It has not become luggage in his mind.

Yes, in the spur of the moment he was angry; he said something, but now the anger is gone, and all that he had said in that moment has gone. He has not become committed to it forever; it was a momentary flare-up, a ripple. But he is not frozen in it; he is a flowing phenomenon. The ripple was there, a wave had arisen; now it is no more. He is not going to carry it always and always. Even if you make him remember it, he will laugh. He will say, "All nonsense!" He will say, "I don't remember. Is it so?" He will say, "Have I really said that? Impossible!" He will say, "How I can say that? You must have imagined it."

It was a flare-up: this must be understood. One who lives moment to moment is sometimes angry, sometimes happy, sometimes sad. But you can depend on him—he will not carry these things forever. A man who is very controlled and does not allow any emotion to arise in his being is very dangerous. If you insult him, he is not angry—he holds it back. By and by, he will accumulate so much anger that he is going to do something really nasty.

There is nothing wrong in a momentary flare of anger—it is beautiful in a way. It simply shows that the person is still alive. A momentary flare-up simply shows that the person is not dead, that he responds to situations and responds authentically. When he feels that the situation is such that anger is needed, anger is there. When he feels that the situation is such that happiness is needed, happiness is there. He goes with the situation. He has no prejudice for or against; he has no ideology as such. He does not have a certain idea that one should not be angry, that whatsoever the situation, one has to remain non-angry.

If a man tries to be non-angry in that way, what will he do? He will repress his anger. Eventually that anger will come all out of proportion in situations where it will look almost mad. He will be capable of murdering somebody, or committing suicide, or doing something really harmful—because when so much anger is released, it is very poisonous, very destructive.

> Nothing is wrong with ordinary anger. In fact, a person who can become angry and forget all about it the next moment is really a very good person.

Nothing is wrong with ordinary anger. In fact, a person who can become angry and forget all about it the next moment is really a very good person. You will always find that person friendly, alive, loving, compassionate. One who is always holding onto his emotions—controlling and controlling and controlling, a person of so-called discipline—is never a good person. He will always show that he is holier than you, but you can see his anger in his eyes. You can see it in his face; you can see it in his every gesture—the way he walks, the way he talks, the way he relates with people—you can always see it there, boiling. He is ready to burst any moment. These are the murderers; these are the criminals; these are the real evildoers. If the person goes on controlling, all his control will make his ego stronger and stronger.

Now, ego is far more dangerous than anger. Anger is human, nothing wrong with it. It is simple: it is simply a situation in which you are provoked, and you are alive, so you respond to it. It is saying that you will not yield; it is saying that this is not a situation you can accept; it is saying that this is a situation in which you want to say no. It is a protest, and nothing is wrong with that. I am not against anger; I am against accumulated anger. I am not against sex; I am against accumulated sexuality.

Anything that is in the moment is good; anything that is carried from the past is bad, is diseased, is illness.

Think Not of the Morrow

This man Hua-tzu became like a child: *Today he would not remember yesterday; tomorrow he would not remember today.*

Jesus says to his disciples, "Think not of the morrow. Look at the lilies in the field, how beautiful they are. They don't think of the past; they don't think of the future. They are not worried at all about what is going to happen and what has happened. They simply live herenow, that is their beauty." That is the beauty of the trees and the rocks and the stars and the rivers. All of existence is beautiful because it has no past.

Man is ugly—his past makes him ugly. Apart from man, nothing is ugly because it is only man who goes on brooding about the past and the future, and goes on missing the life that is available in the present. That is the only life there is, the only dance there is. Naturally, you become ugly because you have no opportunity to live, to live authentically.

I have heard a beautiful anecdote:

A man was talking with his friend, the tailor, about hunting trips.

"Once," said the tailor, "I was in Africa hunting lions. I discovered one standing ten feet away—and there I was without my gun. The lion came closer. Now he was only five feet away."

"What happened?" the man asked breathlessly.

"Well, to make a long story short, he leaped up and killed me."

"What? What do you mean he killed you?" the man asked. "You're sitting here, very much alive."

"Ha!" said the tailor. "You call this living?"

Even people who look alive are not really alive. They have been killed, and not once, but many times. Killed by the past, the lion of the past; killed by the future, the lion of the future. And they are being killed every day; they are being murdered every day by these two enemies.

There is a beautiful Buddhist parable of many meanings. All the meanings are beautiful, but today try to understand one certain meaning in it:

In a forest a man is running, trying to escape from a lion who is following him, chasing him. The man comes to a precipice. There is no other way to go, so he stops. For a single moment he cannot understand what to do. He looks down. It is a very deep valley, a great abyss. If he jumps, he is gone. But still there is a possibility for him—miracles happen. So he looks down more closely, and there, deep in the valley, two more lions are standing, looking up. So that possibility is gone.

The lion is coming closer, and he is roaring; the man can hear the roar. His only possibility is to hang from the roots of a tree sticking out over the valley. He cannot jump and he cannot stand on the precipice, so he holds onto the roots of the tree. The roots are very fragile, and he is afraid that at any moment they will break. Not only that, it is a very cold evening; night is gathering, and the sun is going down. And his hands are so cold that he is afraid he will not be able to hold on for long. Already the roots are slipping out of his hands. They are frozen. Death is certain. Each moment, death is there.

Then he looks up. Two mice are chewing through the roots of the tree. One is white and one is black: the symbol of day and night, the symbol of time. Time is running out fast, and the two mice are chewing through the roots, and they are really doing a great job. They are almost at the end; they are just going to finish—it is evening, and they also have to go and rest, so they are finishing in a hurry. Any moment the root will break away from the tree.

The man looks up again, and there on the tree is a beehive out of which honey is dripping. He forgets all, and tries to catch a drop on his tongue. And he succeeds. The taste is really sweet.

Now, this parable has many meanings. I have talked about this parable in different ways. This time I would like to indicate a certain meaning: *this moment.* In the past, a lion is coming; in the future two lions are waiting. Time is running out fast, death is very close by—as it is always. Day and night, the two mice, are cutting away the very roots of life—but still, if you can live in the present, the taste is tremendously sweet.

It is really beautiful. The man lived in the moment and forgot everything. For the moment there was no death, no lions, no time, nothing existed—only the sweet taste of honey on his tongue.

This is the way to live; this is the only way to live. Otherwise, you will not be living. This is the situation each moment.

The parable is really very existential. This is the situation: you are the person clinging to the root of the tree, surrounded from everywhere by death, and time is running short. Any moment you will drop into death and disappear. Now what to do? Worry about the past? Worry about the future? Worry about death? Worry about time? Or enjoy this moment?

"Think not of the morrow" means to let this moment become a drop of sweet honey on your tongue. Even though death is always there, life is beautiful. Even though the past was not very good, and who knows about the future?—it may not be very good. As things are, it is hopeless to hope—but this moment is beautiful. Look at this moment. Let me become a drop of honey on your tongue. This moment is tremendously beautiful. What is missing? What is lacking?

Healthy and Whole

If you can be in this moment—that is the meaning of the Taoist expression. Hua-tzu *lost his memory.*

His family were troubled about it and invited a diviner to tell his fortune, but without success. They invited a shaman to perform an auspicious rite, but it made no difference. They invited a doctor to treat him, but it did no good.

Now, that is beautiful—and meaningful. It was not a disease, so no doctor could cure it. Had it been a disease, then the doctor could have cured it. It was not anything physical. The man was perfectly healthy. In fact, he had never been healthier than he must have been at that time. When you forget about your past, you forget all about your illnesses also. The past is a reservoir of all illnesses.

When you forget the past, you are neither young nor old, you simply are. And that is the moment of being healthy and whole.

The man must have been very healthy, so what could doctors

do? The family called the doctors, but they could not treat him. It was not a disease.

A disease could have been treated, but this was not a disease. The family asked a diviner to tell his fortune, but without success, because a man who has no memory has no imagination for the future, and a man who has no imagination for the future is un-predictable. You cannot predict anything about him—he is just open.

Ordinarily, people are predictable because they have a cer-tain projection into the future, some idea about the future, a seed for the future. That seed will one day sprout. That's how the diviners, the palmists, the fortune-tellers live: they live on your imagination. If you go to a fortune-teller, he will look at your hand, and he will say, "There is a great possibility that money will come—but it will not stay." It can be said about anybody— "Money will come." Everybody is hoping for it, so who is going to deny that it will come? That's why the person has come to the fortune-teller, for his ideas to be approved, to be confirmed.

Money will come, but he will not be able to keep it—who has ever been able to keep money? Money comes and goes. In fact, money exists only in its coming and going. If you are able to keep it, it is no longer money. You can keep a thousand notes in your house, you can hoard it underground, but it is no longer money. You could have kept stones there; it would have been just the same. Money exists only in its coming and going.

When somebody gives you a hundred-dollar note, when the note changes hands, then it is money. Just for a moment it is money—when it changes hands. Then the other person is getting something out of it, and you are getting something out of it. When you give it to somebody else, again it will be money. That's why notes are called *currency*. "Currency" means "movement." They should move. The more they move, the more money there is.

That's why there is more money in America and less in poorer countries: there is so much movement. Everybody is just spending—spending what they have, and spending even that which they hope they will have one day. People are purchasing cars and fridges and everything on credit. Someday they hope they will have the money, and then they will pay, but they are purchasing right now. There is money in America because people have come to know that money exists in its movement. Let the money change hands—the more it changes hands, the richer and richer and richer the country becomes.

Let a one-hundred-rupee note circulate here. If we are five hundred people, and a one-hundred-rupee note changes hands, it becomes five hundred notes of one hundred rupees. Each time it comes to one person, that person will have one hundred rupees. But let one person keep the note, and then this group will be poor. Then only one person has a hundred-rupee note. If it had changed hands and moved, then everybody would have enjoyed a hundred rupees. Of course, there would have been much wealth.

But these astrologers' predictions are possible only about people who have an idea of a future. This is significant: people who live below the mind are predictable. People who live in the mind are predictable because they are mechanical. You can say what they will do tomorrow because they will repeat themselves. Nothing new is going to happen; they will simply repeat their past.

But one who has gone beyond mind is unpredictable because he will never repeat anything. So you cannot use any clue from his past to predict his actions. The diviners failed; they could not say anything about Hua-tzu. And the shaman was called, but he also could not do anything. The shaman can only do one thing: he can pray. He can do certain rituals to help. But one who has gone beyond mind needs no prayer; no prayer will be of any help to him. In fact, prayer means asking God to do something, naturally—asking God to do something for you. One who has gone beyond mind has become part of God: there is nobody to pray and nobody to be prayed to. Who is there to ask? Only God is.

No, these auspicious rites and rituals were of no help. So nobody could help.

There was a Confucian of Lu who, acting as his own go-between, claimed that he could cure it. Hua-tzu's wife and children offered half of their property in return for his skill.

Punishment and Reward

Confucians are the first behaviorists of the world. Pavlov and B. F. Skinner are nothing but their disciples. Confucius says that a man's behavior can be changed, manipulated, through punishment and reward. That is the whole technique that has been used down the ages by the moralists. You reward the child if he follows your idea; you punish him if he goes against you. Through punishment and reward, by and by you condition his mind.

All minds are conditioned—and what Maoists are doing in China is very ancient; Confucius taught it very well. The idea must be understood: that a person can be manipulated if you torture him or you reward him. Through greed and fear, a person can be manipulated.

That's what you have been doing to your children; that's what has been done to you by your parents and by your society.

What are you doing to criminals in your prisons? Torturing them, trying to condition their minds. Why does the priest go on talking about hell and heaven; what is the idea of hell and heaven? It is just the simple idea of punishment and reward. If you follow the priest, you will be rewarded in heaven; if you don't follow the priest, you will be punished in hell. And they have painted hell in such colors that anybody will become afraid, anybody will start trembling. Then one starts holding on to oneself, repressing oneself.

This Confucian said he could cure Hua-tzu. First of all, the man was not ill, so to say that he could be cured is stupid. The same stupidity continues, even now. There are many people in Western countries who are not mad but who are being "cured" by psychologists. They are not mad; in fact, they have gone a little higher than ordinary people. They are what Sufis call *mastas*, those who have become *mast*, or drunk with God. But they are being treated—and what is their treatment? Electroshock, beating, torturing in a thousand and one ways. Electroshock treatment is a torture—a modern invention to torture man.

Or these people are put into asylums and forced to live a very routine life. Many of them are farther ahead than ordinary humanity; many of them have achieved a better consciousness. But naturally they have fallen separate from ordinary humanity.

The normal seems to be the rule; the normal seems to be the healthy person. The normal is not the norm, remember; the normal simply means the crowd, the mob, the mass. The mass is not healthy, and the mass is not in any way sane; in fact, no individual has ever been as insane as the behavior of masses prove.

Masses are more insane—no Hindu is as insane as the Hindu society. No Muslim is as insane as the Muslim society. The Muslim mob can go and burn a temple and kill Hindus, but ask each individual of that crowd, and you will not find any individual who is so insane. Every individual will say that "somehow it happened." He was just there, and he somehow joined in with the crowd: "It was not good." Ask each individual, and you will be told, "It was not good." But the crowd did it. The crowd has always been insane. Wars, conflicts between religions and nations—these are all just crowd minds.

The crowd mind is insane. The psychologists and the psychiatrists and the psychoanalysts try to adjust the person if he goes a little beyond society. If Freud had been available, Hua-tzu would have been psychoanalyzed. If Skinner had been there, he would have been reconditioned. That's what this Confucian said.

The Confucian told them: "This is clearly not a disease which can be divined by hexagrams and omens, or charmed away by auspicious prayers, or treated by medicine and the needle. I shall try reforming his mind, changing his thoughts. There is a good chance that he will recover."

He said that he would recondition, re-form; he would recondition Hua-tzu's mind. How do you recondition a mind? You start torturing the body. When the body is tortured, the consciousness that was flying beyond has to come down to look after the body, naturally. You exist in the body; the body is your vehicle. If your body is harmed, you naturally cannot fly very high; you have to come back to protect your body. That's the way to recondition. And that's what he did.

Then the Confucian tried stripping Hua-tzu . . .

It may have been winter, and he stripped Hua-tzu naked; naturally, when he started shivering, his mind would suddenly come back: "You are shivering, Hua-tzu. Find your clothes." And he would start looking for his clothes.

. . . and he looked for his clothes; tried starving him, and he looked for food; tried shutting him up in the dark, and he looked for light.

His consciousness was flowing higher than the mind. If you torture the body, the consciousness has to come back to the body. Have you noticed it? If a small thorn enters your foot, your consciousness will go there. A small thorn in your foot, and your consciousness has to go there; it is a safety measure. Otherwise, the thorn will become poisonous, will become septic. It is part of your life-survival mechanism that consciousness has to go there and look after it and take the thorn out. When the thorn is there, you forget everything else. Haven't you noticed it? If your teeth hurt, you forget everything else. Then your whole consciousness gathers around your teeth. That pain must be tackled first. When you have a headache then everything else is forgotten. Somebody may be playing beautiful music, but you cannot hear it. Somebody may be dancing, but you cannot look at it. There may be beauty all around, but how can you look at the beauty? You are not free. Your headache is pulling you down into the body.

This is what the Confucian follower did. He starved the man, stripped him naked, put him in the dark—naturally he started looking for light, looking for warmth, for clothes, for food.

The Confucian was delighted and told the man's sons:

"The sickness is curable, but my arts have been passed down secretly through generations and are not disclosed to outsiders—so I shall shut out his attendants and stay alone with him in his room for seven days."

They agreed . . .

The art is not much of a secret. The art is simply to threaten the man with death—either to beat him or to jump on his chest with a spear. So the man is threatened with death. In that moment, he has to come back to his body. When one comes to one's body, the mind starts functioning again because mind is part of the body. The mind is a subtle mechanism of the body.

This man, Hua-tzu, had lost his contact with his mind, but the mind was there—the mind is always there. Even when a person goes beyond mind, the mind remains there, dormant, sleepy, in the body. If you are pulled back into the body, the mind is stirred again and starts functioning.

They agreed, and no one knew what methods the Confucian used, but the sickness of many years was completely dispelled in a single morning.

When Hua-tzu woke up he was very angry.

In fact, he was awake all this time, but now he has fallen asleep. But to the Confucian mind, or to the ordinary mind of humanity, it seems as if he woke up, as if he had been asleep. "When Hua-tzu woke up he was very angry." Naturally, what is sleep to us was not sleep to him.

It used to happen in Ramakrishna's case. Singing the song of Kali, dancing before Kali, many times he would fall and become unconscious. He would be unconscious to us, but to himself he would be superbly conscious. From the outside it looked like he was in a coma. If you had asked psychoanalysts, they would have said this was hysteria, a hysterical fit.

If you ask the psychiatrist about Ramakrishna, he will prove that he was neurotic. They did the same to Jesus, so they could not leave Ramakrishna alone. Jesus was neurotic, they say. Ramakrishna would have been even more neurotic to them. Sometimes for six days he would remain unconscious—unconscious to us. Let me remind you again and again: to himself he was superbly conscious. In fact, he was so conscious within himself that his whole consciousness was involved there; all consciousness was taken from the outside to the inside, it came to the center. That's why on the outside he appeared unconscious.

You are conscious on the outside because inside you are unconscious. In the deepest core of your being you are fast asleep and snoring; that's why you look so awake on the outside. Things change. When a man like Ramakrishna moves into his core from the outside, he falls asleep on the outside, and inside he becomes awake. To us it would seem that he has forgotten all; to him, it seems he has remembered all.

When Hua-tzu woke up he was very angry. The same used to happen to Ramakrishna. People would try to bring him back. Naturally, the disciples would become very afraid—would he come back or not? And they would massage his feet with ghee and camphor, and they would massage his head and his whole body, and they would try to bring him back somehow. Sometimes the disciples would even do something that looks ugly and cruel. They would suffocate him by closing his nose, because when the body is suffocated and a great need for air arises, the consciousness has to come back.

Or sometimes they would burn very bitter things around him, and the smoke would get into his nose and he would suffer terribly. He would start moving, moaning, and then he would come back. And these were disciples, not enemies! Sometimes you can do harm even while thinking you are doing good.

When he came back he would start crying and the disciples would ask, "Why are you crying?" He would say, "What have you done? Why have you brought me back? I was so tremendously happy inside. I was in a totally different world. I was in the world of God. God was very much present. I was showered by bliss. Why have you brought me back? Let me go again."

When Hua-tzu woke up he was very angry. Naturally. Obviously.

He dismissed his wife, punished his sons, and chased away the Confucian with a spear.

Maybe that was the same spear that the Confucian had used to threaten him to death.

The authorities of Sung arrested him and wanted to know the reason.

"Formerly, when I forgot," said Hua-tzu, "I was boundless; I did not notice whether heaven and earth existed or not. Now suddenly I remember, and all the disasters and recoveries, gains and losses, joys and sorrows, loves and hates of twenty or thirty years past rise up in a thousand tangled threads. I fear that all the disasters and recoveries, gains and losses, joys and sorrows, loves and hates still to come will confound my heart just as much. Shall I never again find a moment of forgetfulness?"

What you think of as remembering is forgetfulness for one who has arrived home. What to you looks like forgetfulness is really remembering for one who has awakened to his soul. Remember this paradox.

The languages are different. You are asleep, but you think this is waking; you think this is a state of awareness. You are mistaken. Therefore, when a person becomes really aware, it seems to you that he has fallen asleep. You are so self-conscious that when a person loses his self and really becomes conscious, you think he has gone mad. It appears as if he is ill.

He has become whole; he has become healthy.

Hua-tzu said, "I was boundless formerly, when I forgot. There was no boundary to me; there was no definition to me. I was all; I was whole; I was one with the universe; nothing separated me. I was in a tremendous unity—*unio mystica*—there was oneness. And it was beautiful, it was a benediction.

"Now suddenly I remember; and all the disasters and recoveries, gains and losses, joys and sorrows, loves and hates of twenty or thirty years past rise up in a thousand tangled threads."

Now I am back to madness. All of my past is again opening its doors. It is a nightmare.

Now he has tasted a few moments of forgetfulness—or self-remembering. Now he is in a state of mind to compare, that's why he is angry. You cannot compare because you have not experienced anything beyond the past, beyond memory, beyond mind. You have never tasted anything, not a single drop, of no-mind. That's why you cannot compare.

This will happen one day if you continue meditating. One day suddenly you will see that you have taken off from the mind. The airport of the mind is left far behind, and you are soaring high in the sky. Then for the first time you will say, "How beautiful life is. How beautiful existence is." You will feel tremendously grateful. Then to come down back to the mind, you will feel as if you are coming back into the madhouse. Memory is a madhouse.

Everything is rising up: *". . . in a thousand tangled threads. I fear that all the disasters and recoveries, gains and losses, joys and sorrows, loves and hates still to come will confound my heart just as much."* This is past, and now the future is coming, and he will be burdened more and more because the past will grow every day.

"Shall I never again find a moment of forgetfulness?"

In that forgetfulness you come home. In that forgetfulness you remember. In that forgetfulness you become aware for the first time. In that forgetfulness you are in the present, herenow. You enter eternity. That forgetfulness is the door to eternity.

To forget means to forget the world; to forget means to forget the nonessential. To forget means to forget the dust and remember the mirror, remember consciousness.

Gurdjieff used to say to his disciples that they were somnambulists—moving, walking, talking in sleep. The first thing to do has nothing to do with morality; it is to shock you into awareness. Gurdjieff's greatest disciple was P. D. Ouspensky. P. D. Ouspensky dedicated his book *In Search of the Miraculous* to his master with these words: "To Gurdjieff, to my master, who has disturbed my sleep forever." Yes, the master is there to disturb your sleep.

Your sleep is nothing but the mind; mind is another name for your sleep. This is the distinction between Confucian thought and Lao Tzuan thought. Confucius is an ordinary moralist, a puritan—one who believes in conditioning people, in disciplining people. Lao Tzu is a rebellious man who believes in taking people beyond all conditionings—unconditioning people.

Only in freedom is godliness possible; only in utter freedom is truth possible. Seek this utter freedom. Destroy conditionings. Destroy, by and by, all the layers that hold you down.

Take off. The whole sky is yours—in fact, not even the sky is limiting.

Enough for today.

5

Casting the First Stone

I f you can love and forgive, then nothing else is needed.

If you cannot forgive, you cannot love; if you cannot love, you cannot forgive.

Only great love knows how to forgive, and only great forgiveness knows how to love; otherwise, everybody has limitations. If you cannot forgive, you will not be able to love. Everybody commits mistakes, that is human. To err is human, to forgive is divine. And the more you

> If you cannot forgive,
> you cannot love;
> if you cannot love,
> you cannot forgive.

forgive, the more you start moving towards the divine; you start transcending humanity. And the higher you reach, the more love becomes possible.

So remember these two things:

Love unconditionally and forgive unconditionally, and you

will not accumulate any karma, you will not accumulate any past. You will not accumulate any bondage around you, and you will not have any barriers to your vision.

Once barriers disappear from the vision, God is everywhere. If you can forgive and love, then you will find him everywhere; wherever you turn he is there. He is not only in the saints, he is in the sinners too. You cannot see him in the sinner because you cannot forgive him. You cannot see him in the ugly person because you cannot forgive him.

Once you start forgiving, the distinction between the sinner and the saint is lost, the distinction between good and bad disappears. There are no more distinctions; you start seeing the one, the distinctionless. There is no man, no woman, no Black, no white, no Indian, no American. There is pure energy, and that pure energy is God.

. . .

Let the Past Be Past

Jesus went unto the Mount of Olives.
And early in the morning he came again into the temple, and
all the people came unto him, and he sat down and taught
them.
And the scribes and Pharisees brought unto him a woman taken
in adultery, and when they had set her in the midst, they

said unto him: "Master, this woman was taken in adultery, in the very act.

"Now Moses in the law commanded us that such should be stoned. What sayest thou?"

This they said, tempting him, that they might have to accuse him. But Jesus stooped down, and with his finger wrote on the ground, as though he heard them not.

So when they continued asking him, he lifted up himself, and said unto them: "He that is without sin among you, let him first cast a stone at her."

And again he stooped down, and wrote on the ground.

And they which heard it, being convicted by their own conscience, went out one by one, beginning at the eldest, even unto the last. And Jesus was left alone, and the woman standing in the midst.

When Jesus had lifted up himself, and saw none but the woman, he said unto her: "Woman, where are those thine accusers? Hath no man condemned thee?"

She said, "No man, Lord." And Jesus said unto her: "Neither do I condemn thee. Go, and sin no more."

—The Bible, John 8

Religion always deteriorates into morality. Morality is dead religion, and religiousness is alive morality; they never meet, they cannot meet because life and death never meet. Light and darkness never meet. But the problem is that they look very alike—

the corpse looks very similar to the living person. Everything is similar to when the person was alive: the same face, the same eyes, the same nose, hair, and body. Just one thing is missing, and that one thing is invisible. Life is missing, but life is not tangible and not visible. So when a man is dead, he looks as if he is still alive. And with the problem of morality, it becomes more complex.

Morality looks exactly like religion, but it is not. It is a corpse; it stinks of death.

Real religion is youth, is freshness—the freshness of flowers and the freshness of the morning dew. Living religion—what I call religiousness—is splendor, the splendor of the stars, of life, of existence itself. When there is religiousness there is no morality at all—and yet the person is moral. But there is no idea of what "morality" is. It is just natural; it follows you as your shadow follows you. You need not carry your shadow; you need not think about your shadow. You need not look back again and again and see whether the shadow is still following you or not. It follows—just like that, morality follows a religious person. You never consider it, you never deliberately think about it; it is your natural flavor.

> Morality looks exactly like religion, but it is not. It is a corpse; it stinks of death.

But when religion is dead, when life has disappeared, then one starts thinking continuously about morality. Consciousness has disappeared, and conscience becomes the only shelter.

Consciousness Is Yours, Conscience Is Borrowed

Conscience is a pseudophenomenon. Consciousness is yours, conscience is borrowed. Conscience is of the society, of the collective mind; it does not arise in your own being. When you are conscious, you act rightly because your act is conscious, and the conscious act can never go wrong. When your eyes are fully open and there is light, you don't try to go through the wall; you go through the door. When there is no light and your eyes are not functioning well, naturally you will grope in the dark. You will have to think a thousand and one times where the door is: "To the left, to the right? Am I moving in the right direction?" You stumble on the furniture, and you try to get out through the wall.

A religious person is one who has eyes to see, who has awareness. In that awareness, your actions are naturally good. Let me repeat: naturally good. Not that you make them good—managed goodness is not goodness at all: it is pseudo; it is pretentious; it is hypocrisy. When goodness is natural, spontaneous, just as trees are green and the sky is blue, so is the religious person moral—completely unaware of his morality, aware of himself but unaware of his morality. He has no idea that he is moral, that he is good, that what he is doing is right.

Out of awareness comes innocence; out of awareness comes the right act—of its own accord. It has not to be brought, it has not to be cultivated, it has not to be practiced. Then morality has a beauty—but it is no longer "morality"; it is simply moral. In fact, it is just a religious way of living.

But when religion has disappeared, then you have to manage it. Then you have to constantly think about what is right and what is wrong. How are you going to decide what is right and what is wrong? You don't have your own eyes to see; you don't have your own heart to feel; you are dead and dull. You don't have your own intelligence to go into things; you have to depend on the collective mind that surrounds you.

Religiousness has one flavor—whether you are Christian or Hindu or Mohammedan does not make any difference—a religious person is simply religious; he is neither Hindu nor Mohammedan nor Christian. But a moral person is not just moral—either he is Hindu or Christian or Mohammedan or Buddhist, because his morality had to be learned from the outside. If you are born in a Buddhist country, in a Buddhist society, you will learn the Buddhist morality. If you are born in a Christian world, you will learn the Christian morality. You will learn from others—and you have to learn from others, because you don't have your own insight.

So morality is borrowed—it is social; it is of the mob; it comes from the masses. And it comes to the masses from where? From tradition: they have heard what is right and what is wrong, and they have carried it down the ages. It is being given from one generation to another. Nobody bothers whether it is a corpse; nobody bothers whether the heart still beats. It goes on being given from one generation to another. It is dull, dead, heavy; it kills joy. It kills celebration; it kills laughter; it makes people ugly; it makes people heavy, monotonous, boring. But it has a long tradition.

Another thing to be remembered: religiousness is always born anew. In Jesus, religion is born again. It is not the same religion that existed with Moses. It has not come from Moses; it has no continuity with the past. It is utterly discontinuous with the past; it arises again and again.

Just like a flower comes on the rosebush, it has nothing to do with the flowers that have come before; it is discontinuous. It comes on its own—it has no past, no history, no biography. For the moment, it is there—so beautifully there, so authentically there. For the moment, it is so strong, so alive, and yet so fragile. In the morning sun it was so young . . . by the evening it will be gone, the petals will start falling onto the earth from which they had come in the first place. It will not leave any trace behind; if you come the next day, it is no longer there. It has not left any marks; it has simply disappeared. As it has come out of nothingness, so it has gone back to nothingness, to the original source.

Religiousness is just like that. When it happens in a Buddha, it is fresh, young, like a roseflower; it disappears, it leaves no traces. Buddha has said: "Religion is like a bird flying in the sky, it leaves no footprints." It happens in a Moses—it is fresh, young again. Then in Jesus—it is fresh and young again. When it happens to you, it will not have any continuity; it will not come from somebody else—from Christ, from Buddha, from me; it will not come from anybody else—it will arise in you, it will bloom in you. It will be a flowering of your being, and then it will be gone.

You cannot give it to anybody; it is not transferable. It cannot be given, cannot be borrowed; it is not a thing. Yes, if somebody wants to learn, it can be learned. If somebody wants to imbibe it, it can be imbibed. When a disciple learns from being around a master, absorbs the vibes of the master, then too, it is something that is happening within the disciple. Maybe the disciple gets the challenge, the provocation, the call, from the outside—but that which arises, arises in you, utterly in you. It does not come from the outside.

It is as if you are not aware that you can sing: you have never tried, you have never thought about the possibility. One day you see a singer, and suddenly his song starts pulsating around you. In a moment of awakening, you become aware that you have also got a throat and a heart. Now, suddenly, for the first time, you become aware that there has been a song hidden in you, and you release it. But the song comes from your innermost core; it arises from your being. Maybe the provocation, the call, came from the outside, but not the song.

So the master is a catalytic agent. His presence provokes something in you; his presence does not function as a cause. Carl Gustav Jung is right in bringing a new concept to the Western world—it has existed in the East for centuries—the concept of synchronicity. There are things that happen as cause and effect, and there are things that don't happen as cause and effect but just by synchronicity. This idea has to be understood because it will help you to understand the difference between morality and religiousness.

Morality is cause and effect. Your father, your mother, have taught you something; they function as the cause, and then the effect continues in you. You will teach your children; you will become the cause, and the effect will continue in your children. But listening to a singer, suddenly you start humming a tune. There is no cause-and-effect relationship. The singer is not the cause, and you are not the effect. You have caused the effect yourself—you are both the cause and the effect. The singer functioned only as a remembrance, the singer functioned only as a catalytic agent.

What has happened to me, I cannot give to you. Not that I don't want to give it to you, no. It cannot be given; its very nature is such that it cannot be given—but I can present it to you, I can make it available to you. Seeing that it is possible, seeing that it has happened to another person, "Why not to me?" Suddenly something clicks inside you. You become alert to a possibility, alert to a door that is in you, but you were never looking at; you had forgotten it. Something starts sprouting in you. I function as a catalytic agent, not as a cause.

Religiousness Is Synchronicity, Morality Is Causal

The concept of synchronicity simply says that one thing can start something somewhere without it being a cause. It says that if somebody plays a sitar in a room where another sitar has been placed in the corner, and if the player is really a master, a maestro, the sitar that is just sitting there in the corner will start throbbing— because of the other sitar being played in the room, the vibe, the whole milieu. The sitar that is just sitting there in the corner— nobody is playing it, nobody is touching it—you can see its strings vibrating, whispering. Something that was hidden is surfacing;

something that was not manifest is manifesting. Religiousness is synchronicity; morality is causal. Morality comes from the outside; religiousness arises in you.

When religiousness disappears, there is only morality, and morality is very dangerous. First, you yourself don't know what is right, but you start pretending; the hypocrite is created. You start pretending, you start showing that whatsoever you are doing is right. You don't know what right is, and naturally, because you don't know, you can only pretend. You will continue doing the same as you were, but from the back door. From the back door you will have one life, and from the front door another. From the front door you may be smiling, and from the back door you may be crying and weeping. From the front door you will pretend to be a saint, and from the back door you will be as much of a sinner as anybody else. Your life will become split.

This is what is creating schizophrenia in the whole human consciousness. You become two or many. Naturally, when you are two, there is constant conflict. Naturally, when you are many, there is a crowd, and a lot of noise, and you can never settle in silence. You can never rest in silence—silence is possible only when you are one, when there is nobody else within you, when you are one piece, not fragmented.

Morality creates schizophrenia, split personalities, divisions. A moral person is not an individual, because he is divided. Only a religious person is an individual. The moral person has a personality but no individuality. "Personality" means a *persona*, a mask—the moral person has many personalities, not just one, because there are many personalities around him. In different situations, different personalities are needed; with different people, different personalities are needed. To one he shows one face, to another he shows another face.

One goes on changing faces. Watch, and you will see how you go on changing faces every moment. Alone you have one face. In your bathroom you have one face, in the office you have another. Have you observed the fact that in your bathroom you become more childish? Sometimes you can stick out your tongue in front of the mirror, or you can make faces, or you can hum a tune, sing a song, or you can even have a little dance in the bathroom.

But if you become aware that your child is looking through the keyhole while you are dancing or sticking out your tongue in front of the mirror, you change—immediately change! The old face comes back, the "father" personality: this cannot be done in front of the child; otherwise, what will he think? That you are also like him? So what about that seriousness that you always show the child? You immediately put on another face; you become serious. The song disappears, the dance disappears, the tongue disappears. You are back into your so-called front-door personality.

Morality creates conflict in you because it creates many faces. The problem is that when you have many faces, you tend to forget which is your original one. With so many faces, how can you remember which is your original one? The Zen masters say that the first thing for a seeker to know is his original face because only then can something start. Only the original face can grow; a mask cannot grow. A false face can have no growth. Growth is possible only for the original face because only the original has life. So the first thing to know is: "What is my original face?" And it is arduous because there is a long queue of false faces, and you are lost in your false faces. Sometimes you may think, "This is my original face." If you go deeply into it, you will find that again this is a false face; maybe it is more ancient than the others, so it looks more original.

Buddha is reported to have said: "Taste me from anywhere and you will find the same taste as when you taste the sea. From this side, from that side, from this shore, from that shore—taste the sea from anywhere, and it is salty." Buddha says: "So is my taste. Taste me while I am asleep; taste me while I am awake; taste me when somebody is insulting me; taste me when somebody is praising me—you will always find the same taste, the taste of a buddha."

The religious person is an individual.

This is a very, very complex phenomenon. A religious person is a totally different person. He will be able to forgive; he will be able to understand. He will be able to see the limitations of human beings and their problems. He will not be so hard and so cruel—he cannot be. His compassion will be infinite.

Be Moral, but Not a Moralist

Before we enter these sutras of Jesus, a few things have to be understood. First: the concept of sin; the concept of the immoral act. What is immoral? How should we define immorality? What is the criterion?

One thing is immoral in India, another thing is immoral in China. That which is immoral in India may be moral in Iran, and that which is moral in Russia may be immoral in India. There are a thousand and one moralities—how to decide? Because now that the world has become a global village, there is a lot of confusion. What is right?

To eat meat is right? Is it moral or immoral? The vegetarian says it is immoral. Many Jainas have come to me and said, "What about Jesus eating meat? How can Jesus be an enlightened person— and you say that he is enlightened—how can he be? He eats meat." For a Jaina it is impossible to conceive that Jesus can be enlightened because he eats meat. Jainas have come to me and asked, "How can Ramakrishna be enlightened? He eats fish. He cannot be." Now they have a very definite criterion with them: vegetarianism.

There are a thousand and one moralities. If you go on trying to decide, you will be in difficulty; it will be impossible for you. You will go mad; you will not be able to eat. You will not be able to sleep; you will not be able to do anything. Now, there is a Jaina sect which is afraid of breathing. To breathe is immoral because with each breath you will kill many small cells living in the air around you. They are right! That's why the doctor has to use a mask, so that he does not go on inhaling things that are moving around, infections. That Jaina sect is afraid to breathe; breathing becomes immoral. Walking becomes immoral—there are Jainas who don't walk in the night because they may kill something in the darkness, an ant or something else. Mahavira never moved at nighttime and never moved in the rainy season because there are many more insects around then. Movement becomes difficult; breathing becomes difficult.

If you go on looking around at all the moralities, you will simply go crazy or you will have to commit suicide. But to commit suicide is immoral! If you listen to all kinds of moralities, it seems to be the logical thing to just commit suicide. That seems to be the least immoral thing. One act and you are finished; there will be no immorality—but that act too is immoral. When you commit suicide you are not dying alone, remember. It is not just killing one person. You have millions of cells in the body that are alive, millions of lives inside you, which will die with you. So you have killed millions of people. When you fast, is it moral or immoral? There are people who say to fast is moral, and there are people who say to fast is immoral. Why?—because when you fast, you kill many cells inside yourself; they die of starvation. If you fast, a kilo of weight disappears every day: you are killing many things inside you. Every day a kilo of weight disappears; within a month you will be just a structure of bones. All those people who used to live inside you—small people—have all died. You have killed all of them.

Or there are people who say to fast is like eating meat. Now, it sounds very strange but it is true, there is a logic to it. When a kilo of weight disappears, where has it gone? You have eaten it! Your body needs that kind of food every day, and you go on replacing it with food from the outside. If you don't replace it with food from the outside, the body still goes on eating because the body needs food every twenty-four hours; the body has to live. It needs a certain fuel; it starts eating its own flesh. To be on a fast is to be a cannibal.

These moralities can drive you mad. There is no way to choose.

What is moral to me? To be aware is moral. What you are doing is not the question. If you are doing it in full awareness, whatsoever it is—it is irrelevant what it is, irrespective of the fact of what it is—if you are doing it in full awareness, it is moral. If you are doing it in unawareness, in unconsciousness, then it is immoral. To me, "morality" means "awareness."

The French language seems to be the only language which has only one word for two words: conscience and consciousness. That seems to be very, very beautiful—consciousness *is* conscience. Ordinarily, consciousness is one thing, and conscience is another thing. Consciousness is yours; conscience is given to you by others, it is a conditioning.

> Become more and more conscious, and you will become more and more moral—you will not become a moralist.

Live by consciousness, become more and more conscious, and you will become more and more moral—you will not become a moralist. You will become moral, and you will not become a moralist. The moralist is an ugly phenomenon.

The Mount of Olives Is Within You

Now the sutras:

Jesus went unto the Mount of Olives.

He always used to go to the mountains whenever he felt that his consciousness was becoming dusty; his mirror was covered with dust. He would go to the mountains in aloneness to cleanse his being, to cleanse his consciousness. It is like when you take a bath, and after the bath you feel your body is fresh, young. Meditation is like an inner bath.

To be alone for a few moments every day is a must; otherwise, you will gather too much dust, and because of that dust your mirror will not reflect any more or will not reflect rightly. It may start distorting things. Haven't you noticed?—a single particle of dust enters your eye, and your vision becomes distorted. The same is true about the inner vision, the inner eye—so much dust goes on collecting there, and the dust comes from relationship. Just like when you travel on a dusty road, you collect dust; when you move with people who are dusty, you collect dust. They are all throwing their dust around; they are all throwing the wrong vibes.

And they cannot do anything about it; they are helpless. I am not saying that you condemn them. What can they do? If you go to a hospital and everybody is ill, and if they are throwing their infections all around, they can't help it. They breathe out, and the infection is released. Haven't you noticed when you go to a hospital to visit somebody?—after just one hour in the hospital, you start feeling a kind of sickness, and you were perfectly healthy when you entered. Just the smell of the hospital, just the faces of the nurses and the doctors, and the medical instruments, and that particular hospital smell, and all the people who are ill, and the whole vibe of illness and death always there. Somebody is always dying. Just being there for one hour and you feel low; a kind of nausea arises in you. Coming out of the hospital, you feel a great relief.

The same is the situation in the world. Everybody is full of anger and violence, aggression, jealousy, possessiveness; everybody is false, pseudo, and everybody is a hypocrite—this is the world. You don't feel it, but when a Jesus moves among you, he feels it because he comes from the heights. He descends from the mountains.

If you go to the Himalayas, and then after living in the Himalayan freshness for a few days you come back to the plains, you feel how dusty, how ugly, how heavy the vibe is. Now you have a comparison. You have seen the fresh waters of the Himalayas, those fresh fountains running forever, and the crystal clear water—and then the municipal tap water! You have the comparison. Only a meditator knows that the world is ill; only a meditator feels that everything is wrong here. When a meditator moves among you, naturally he feels much more dust collecting on him than you can feel because you have lost all sensitivity. You have forgotten that you are a mirror. You know that you are just a dust collector. Only a meditator knows that he is a mirror.

So Jesus goes again and again to the mountains.

Jesus went, unto the mountains, unto the Mount of Olives.

And early in the morning he came again into the temple, and all the people came unto him, and he sat down and taught them.

Only when you have been to the mountains—and that does not mean that you really have to go to the mountains; it is not an outer phenomenon. The Mount of Olives is within you. If you can be alone, if you can forget the whole world for a few seconds, you will regain your freshness. Only then can you go to the temple because only then you *are* a temple. Only then will your presence in the temple be a real presence; there will be a harmony between you and the temple.

Remember, unless you bring your temple to the temple, there is no temple. If you simply go to the temple and don't bring your temple there within you, it is just a house. When Jesus goes into a house, it becomes a temple; when you go into a temple, it becomes a house—because we carry our temples inside. Wherever Jesus goes, it becomes a temple; his presence creates that sacred quality. Only when you bring the temple and the freshness of the mountains and the virginity of the mountains, only then can you teach. You can teach only then, when you have it.

And early in the morning he came again into the temple, and all the people came unto him, and he sat down and taught them.

And the scribes and Pharisees brought unto him a woman taken in adultery, and when they had set her in the midst, they said unto him: "Master, this woman was taken in adultery, in the very act."

Now Moses in the law commanded us, that such should be stoned, but what sayest thou?

This is one of the most important parables in Jesus's life. Go into it slowly, delicately, carefully.

And the scribes and Pharisees . . . Now for that, you can read "the moralists and the puritans." In those days, those were the

Casting the First Stone

names of the moralists—the pundits, the scholars—the scribes and the Pharisees. The Pharisees were the people who were very respectable. On the surface very moral, pretentious, with great egos. "We are moral, and everybody else is immoral"—and always searching and looking into other people's faults. Their whole life was concerned with how to exaggerate their own qualities and reduce others' qualities to nil.

The puritans, the moralists, *brought unto him a woman taken in adultery.*

Now, when you come to a man like Jesus, you have to come there in humbleness. You have to come there to learn something; you have to come there to imbibe something; it is a rare opportunity. And now, here come these fools, and they bring a woman. They bring their ordinary mind—their mediocre mind, their stupidities—with them.

And the scribes and Pharisees brought unto him a woman taken in adultery.

They have not even learned the simple lesson that when you go to a man like Jesus or Buddha, you go to partake, to participate in his consciousness; you go to become intimate with him. You don't bring the ordinary problems of life there; they are irrelevant. That will be wasting a great opportunity. That will be wasting Jesus's time—and he didn't have much time, only three years of ministry. These fools were wasting time like this! But they had a certain strategy; it was a trap. They were not really concerned about the woman. They were creating a trap for Jesus. It was a very calculating act.

And the scribes and Pharisees brought unto him a woman taken in adultery, and when they had set her in the midst, they said unto him: "Master, this woman was taken in adultery, in the very act."

Now, what is adultery? A conscious mind will say that if you don't love a man—maybe the man is your own husband—if you don't love the man, and you sleep with the man, it is adultery. If you don't love the woman—and she may be your own wife—if you don't love her, and you sleep with her, you are exploiting her; you are deceiving her. It is adultery. But that is not the definition of the Pharisees and the puritans, the scribes and the pundits. Their definition is legal; their definition does not arise out of consciousness or love. Their definition arises out of the court. If the woman is not your wife, and you have been found sleeping with her, it is adultery. It is just a legal matter, technical. The heart is not taken into account, only the law. You may be deeply in love with the man or with the woman, but that is not to be taken into account.

The unconscious mind cannot take higher things into account. It can only take the lowest into account. The problem is always legal: is it your woman, your wife? Are you legally wed to her? Then it is good, it is no longer a sin. If she is not your wife, if you are not legally wed to her . . . You may be deeply in love, and you may have immense respect for the woman— you may almost be a worshipper of her, but it is a sin, it is adultery.

Those people brought this woman to Jesus, and *said unto him: "Master, this woman was taken in adultery, in the very act."*

Just the other day I was reading the memoirs of an English Christian missionary who went to Japan in the early days of this century. He was taken around Tokyo. His host had taken him around to show him the city. In one public bath there were men and women bathing in the nude. The missionary was very shocked.

He stood there for five minutes, watched everything, and then said to his host, "Isn't it immoral—women and men bathing naked in a public place?"

The host said, "Sir, this is not immoral in our country. But, sorry to say, to stand here and watch is immoral. I am feeling very guilty standing with you, because it is their business if they want to take a bath naked. That is their freedom. But why are you standing here watching them? That is ugly, immoral." Now, the missionary's standpoint is very ordinary, and the host's standpoint is extraordinary. These people say: *"Master, this woman was taken in adultery, in the very act."*

And what were you doing there? Were you Peeping Toms? What type of people are you? What were you doing there? Why should you be concerned? This woman's life is her life; how she wants to spend her life is her concern—who are you to interfere?

But the puritan and the moralist have always interfered in other people's lives. They are not democratic; they are very dictatorial. They want to control people, condemn people. Now, what were those people doing there? And they say: *"Master, this woman was taken in adultery, in the very act."* They have caught the woman while she was making love.

"Boys Will Be Boys"

One more thing: where is the man? Was she committing adultery alone? Nobody has ever asked this question about this parable. I have read many Christian books, but nobody has ever asked, "Where is the man?" But it is a man's society. It is always the woman who is wrong, not the man. The man will just go free. He may be a Pharisee himself, he may be a respectable man— but the woman has to be condemned.

Haven't you observed? Prostitutes are condemned, but where are the customers? Where are those people? They may be the same people who condemn the prostitutes.

Puritans are always ugly people. They don't live, and they don't allow anybody else to live.

Their only joy is in how to kill other people's joy, how to kill everybody's celebration. Now, what were those people doing there? Didn't they have anything else to do? Didn't they have their own women to love? What kind of people were they? They must have been a little perverted to go out searching and seeking someone who was committing adultery.

And where was the man?

It is always the woman who is condemned—because the woman is a woman, and the man is the dominant one, and all the legal codes have been made by men. They are very prejudicial, biased. All the legal courts say what should be done to a woman if she is found committing adultery, but they don't say anything about what should be done to the man. No, they say, "Boys are boys, and boys will be boys." It is always a question of the woman. Even if a man rapes a woman, the woman is condemned; she loses respect, not the rapist. This is an ugly state of affairs. This can't be called religious; it is very political—basically in men's favor and against women.

All your so-called moralities have been that way. In India, when a husband died, the wife had to go with him into the funeral pyre, only then was she thought to be virtuous. She had to become a *sati*, she had to die with her husband. If she did not die, that meant she was not virtuous. That simply meant she wanted to live without the husband—or maybe she wanted the husband to die! Now she wanted freedom; now she could fall in love with somebody else. In India, it has been thought that there is no life for the woman once the husband has died. Her husband has been her whole life; if the husband goes, she has to go.

But nothing is said about the man if his wife dies—there is no prescription for him that he should die with the woman; no, that isn't a problem. Immediately after the woman has died . . . in India it happens every day; the people cremate the woman and, coming back home, they start thinking about a new marriage:

where and how can the man find a new woman? Not a single day is to be lost. For the man there is one morality, for the woman it is different. It is an unconscious morality and an immoral one.

My definition of morality is that of consciousness, and consciousness is neither man nor woman. Consciousness is just consciousness. Only when something is decided by your being conscious will it be classless, will it be beyond the distinctions of body, caste, creed. Only then is it moral.

Master, they say, this woman was taken in adultery, in the very act. Now Moses in the law commanded us that such should be stoned. But what sayest thou?

This they said, tempting him, that they might have to accuse him. But Jesus stooped down, and with his finger wrote on the ground, as though he heard them not.

This was the trap. They wanted to trap Jesus: "Moses has said that such a woman should be stoned." Nothing is said about the man. Such a woman should be stoned to death; Moses has said this. Now they are creating a problem for Jesus. If Jesus says, "Yes, do as Moses says," they can accuse him because he has always been talking about love, compassion, kindness, forgiveness. They can say, "What about your compassion? What about your forgiveness? What about your love? You say this woman has to be killed by stoning? This is hard and cruel and violent." Tricky fellows.

If Jesus says, "This is not right. Moses is not right," they can say, "So you have come to destroy Moses? So you have come to destroy and corrupt our religion? And you have been saying to people, 'I have not come to destroy but to fulfill.' What about that? If you have come to fulfill, then follow Moses's law." Now they are creating a dilemma. This is the trap. They are not concerned about the woman; remember: their real target is Jesus; the woman is just an excuse. And they have brought such a case . . . that's why they say *in the very act,* red-handed. So it is not a question of deciding whether the woman has really committed adultery.

Otherwise, Jesus would have an excuse to get out. He would say, "First, try to find out whether it really has happened. Bring the witnesses. Let it first be decided." It would take years. So they say, "Red-handed! We have caught her in the very act. We are all witnesses, so there is no question of deciding anything else. The law is clear; Moses has said that such a woman should be stoned." . . . *what sayest thou?* Do you agree with Moses? If you agree, then what about your love and compassion—your whole message? If you don't agree, what do you mean when you say 'I have come to fulfill'? Then you have come to destroy the law of Moses. So, do you think you are higher than Moses? Do you think that you know more than Moses?"

. . . *what sayest thou? This they said, tempting him, that they might have to accuse him. But Jesus stooped down, and with his finger wrote on the ground, as though he heard them not.*

Why? Why did Jesus stoop down? Why did he start writing on the ground? They were just on the bank of a river. Jesus was sitting on the sand. Why did he start writing in the sand? What had happened?

There is one thing to be understood: it is always a delicate problem. For example, if I see that something stated by Buddha is wrong, there is a great hesitation to say that he is wrong. He cannot be wrong. Tradition must have misinterpreted him; something must have been wrongly put into his mouth. Buddha cannot be wrong. But now there is no way to decide, because the scriptures say this clearly. Jesus hesitating . . . Jesus is concerned. He does not want to say a single word against Moses, but he has to, hence the hesitation. He does not want to say anything against Moses, because Moses could not have said it that way. It is his inner feeling that Moses could not have said it that way. But the inner feeling cannot be decisive. These people will say, "Who are you? Why should we care about your inner feeling? We have the written code with us, given by our forefathers. It is there, written clearly!"

Jesus does not want to say anything against Moses because he really has come to fulfill Moses. Anybody who becomes enlightened in the world is always fulfilling all the enlightened ones that have preceded him. Even if sometimes he says something against them, then too he is fulfilling them, because he cannot say anything against them. If you feel that he is saying something against them, then he is saying something against the tradition, against the scripture. But that looks as if he is saying something against Moses, against Buddha, against Abraham. Hence, Jesus stoops down. He starts looking at the sand and starts writing. He is puzzled as to what to do. He has to find a way out. He has to find a way out, in such a way that he does not say anything against

Moses, and yet he cancels the whole law. He really comes with a very miraculous answer, a magical answer.

So when they continued asking him, he lifted up himself, and said unto them: "He that is without sin among you, let him first cast a stone at her."

It is really incredible, it is beautiful—that was his hesitation. He has found a golden mean. He has not said a single word against Moses, and he has not supported Moses either. This is the delicate point to understand. Jesus was really utterly intelligent—uneducated but utterly intelligent, a man of immense awareness. That's why he could find the way out.

He says: *He that is without sin among you* . . . He says, "Perfectly right"—does not say directly that Moses is right, but he says, "Perfectly right. If Moses says so, then it must be so. But then, who should start throwing stones at this woman?"

. . . *He that is without sin among you, let him first cast a stone at her.*

"So start, but only those who are without sin . . ." Now, this is something new that Jesus brings in. You can judge only if you are without sin. You can punish only if you are without sin. If you are also in the same boat, what is the point? Who is going to punish whom?

And again he stooped down and wrote on the ground.

Why did he stoop down again?—because he must have been afraid that there is always the possibility of some foolish person . . . He knows that everybody has committed one sin or another. If they have not committed one, they have been thinking to commit one, which is almost the same. Whether you think or you act makes no difference.

Remember, the difference between sin and crime is this: crime has to be acted out, only then is it crime. You can go on thinking, but if you don't commit it to action, no court can punish you because it never becomes a crime. Only crime is within the jurisdiction of the court, not sin. Then what is sin? Sin is if you think, "I would like to murder this man." No court can do anything. You can say, "Yes, I have been thinking about it my whole life." But thinking is beyond the court's jurisdiction. You are allowed to think. No court can punish you because you dreamt that you killed somebody. You can dream every day, and go on killing as many people as you want. No court can hold you unless it comes to actuality, unless thought becomes deed, unless thought is translated into reality. If it comes out of you and affects society, it becomes a crime.

But it is sin, because God can go on reading your thoughts. There is no need for him to read your acts. The magistrate has to read your acts; he cannot read your thoughts; he is not a thought-reader or a mind reader. But for God there is no difference; whether you think or you do, it is all the same. The moment you think, you have done it.

So Jesus says: *He that is without sin among you*—not without crime. He says: *He that is without sin among you, let him first cast a stone at her.* That distinction was known down the ages—that if you think it, you have committed a sin already.

And again he stooped down . . . Why this time? Because if he goes on looking at the people, his very look may be provocative. If he goes on looking at the people, somebody, just from his look, and out of taking offense, may throw a stone at the poor woman. He does not want to offend; he withdraws. He simply stoops down, starts writing in the sand—again as if he is not there. He becomes absent because his presence can be dangerous. If they have come just to trap him, and he is there and they feel his presence, it will be difficult for them to feel their own consciences, their own consciousnesses. He withdraws into himself; he allows them total freedom to think about it.

He does not interfere. His presence can be an interference; if he goes on looking at them, that will offend their egos. It will also be difficult for them to escape, because it will feel bad to them. Somebody was standing just in next to the mayor of the town or somebody else, the respectable people . . . How can the mayor escape when Jesus is looking at him? If he escapes and does not throw a stone at the woman, it will be proof that he is a sinner. So Jesus stoops down again, starts writing in the sand, gives them a chance—if they want to escape, they can.

And they which heard it, being convicted by their own conscience . . .

Jesus leaves them alone. That is the beauty of the man. He does not even interfere by his presence; he is simply no longer there. Their own consciences start pricking. They know. Maybe they have lusted after this woman many times, or maybe in the past they themselves have participated with this woman. Maybe the woman is a prostitute, and all these respectable people in their turn have made love to her. Because one prostitute means that almost the whole town can become involved.

In India, in the ancient days, prostitutes were called *nagarvadhu*: the wife of the town. That is the right name. All of those people must have been involved in some way or other with this woman or with other women, if not in acts, then in thoughts. My feeling is, it must have been evening and the sun was setting; it was becoming dark, and Jesus was stooping down, writing in the sand, and as it became dark, by and by the people started disappearing.

And they which heard it, being convicted by their own conscience, went out one by one, beginning at the eldest—the mayor!—*even unto the last.*

Convicted by Their Own Conscience

First the eldest disappeared, because of course, they have lived the longest, so they have sinned the longest. The young people may not have been such great sinners; they haven't had enough time yet. But the eldest disappeared first. Those who were standing in front must have moved slowly to the back and escaped— because this man had really created a great problem; he had changed the whole situation. They had come to trap him, and now they were trapped! You cannot trap a Jesus or a Buddha; it is impossible—you will be trapped. You exist at a lower state of mind; how can you trap a higher state of mind? That is just foolish. The higher state can trap you immediately because from that higher state your whole being is available.

Now, Jesus must have looked into those people's consciences—that was possible for him—he must have seen all kinds of sins raising their heads. In fact, even standing there, they were thinking about the woman and how to catch her. Maybe they were angry because somebody else had committed the sin, and they were not given the opportunity. Maybe they were only jealous; maybe they wanted to be there instead of the man, who had not been brought. Jesus must have looked from his height into their hearts. He had trapped them. They had forgotten their trap completely, they had forgotten about Moses and the law, etcetera.

In fact, they were never worried about Moses and the law. This also has to be understood. They were really more interested in stoning the woman, enjoying this murder. Not that they were interested in punishing somebody who had committed a sin—that was just an excuse. They could not leave this opportunity of murdering her—now, Moses can be used. There are a thousand and one things said by Moses; they are not worried about them. They are not interested in all those sayings and all those statements, they are interested in this: "Moses says you can stone a woman if you catch her committing adultery." They can't miss this great opportunity of murder, of violence.

When violence can be committed according to the law, who would like to miss it? Not only will they enjoy the violence, they will enjoy that they are very, very legal people, virtuous followers of Moses.

But now, they have forgotten all about it. Just a little turning by Jesus, and they have forgotten about Moses. Jesus has changed the whole point. He has turned their minds from the woman to themselves. He has converted them; he has turned them around—a one hundred and eighty degree turn. They were thinking about the woman and Moses and Jesus, and he has changed their whole attitude. He has made them their own target. He has turned their consciousness.

Now he says, "Look into yourself. If you have never committed a sin, then . . . then you are allowed, then you can kill this woman."

When Jesus had lifted up himself . . . he saw that they had all gone. And Jesus was left alone, and the woman standing in the midst . . . and he said unto her: "Woman, where are those thine accusers?"

> The moralist is always condemning, accusing; the religious man always accepting, forgiving.

Now he is not saying, "I am accusing you"—*where are those thine accusers?* He is not for a single moment a participant in it. He has not judged; he has not condemned. He has not said a single thing to the woman. He simply says: *"Woman, where are those thine accusers? Hath no man condemned thee?"*

Have they all gone? Has any man thrown a stone at you?

She said, "No man, Lord."

She must have felt a deep respect, reverence, for this man who has not only saved her physically, but who has not even accused her in any way. Spiritually he has also saved her. She must have looked into those eyes, which have only love and compassion and nothing else. This is the religious man.

The moralist is always condemning, accusing; the religious man always accepting, forgiving.

She said, *"No man, Lord. And Jesus said unto her: Neither do I condemn thee. Go, and sin no more."*

Jesus says, "There is nothing to be worried about—the past. The past is past; gone is gone. Forget about it. But take some lessons from this situation. Don't go on making the same mistakes in the future—if you think they are mistakes. I am not accusing you."

Neither do I condemn thee . . . But if you feel that you have done something wrong, then it is up to you. Don't do it again. Forget the past, and don't go on repeating it."

That is the whole message of all the buddhas and all the christs and all the krishnas: forget the past, and if you understand, don't do it again. That's enough. There is no punishment; there is no judgment. If you have been doing something, you were helpless. You are unconscious; you have your limitations. You have your desires, unfulfilled desires. Whatsoever you have been doing was the only thing you could have done. So what is the point of accusing and condemning you? The only thing that can be done is that your consciousness can be raised high.

That woman must have moved into a higher consciousness. She must have been afraid that she was going to be killed. This man, by a single statement, saved her from death. Not only that, the accusers disappeared. This man did a miracle. Not only did they not kill her, they simply became ashamed and escaped like thieves into the darkness of the night. This man is a magician.

Now, he is saying, "I don't condemn you. If you feel you have been doing something wrong, don't do it again. That's enough." He has converted her.

This is what people on LSD call a "contact high." Jesus is high; if you come in close affinity with him, you will start moving higher. This is synchronicity—noncausal. The woman must have come there almost condemning herself, ashamed of herself, thinking of committing suicide. He has raised that woman, transformed that woman.

She said, "No man, Lord" . . . Jesus becomes Lord; Jesus becomes God to her. She has never seen such a godly man before. With no condemnation, one becomes a god. With no judgment, one becomes a god. Just his presence, a single statement, and those people disappeared and she was saved. Not only saved physically, but spiritually intact. Jesus has not interfered at all. He has not condemned; he has not said a single word. He simply says, "Don't repeat your past"—not a single word more. "Let the past be past and the gone, gone. You become new. All is good, and you are forgiven."

Jesus transformed many people by forgiving them. That was one of the accusations against him: "He forgives people. Who is he to forgive? Somebody has committed a sin—the society has to punish him! If society cannot punish him and he escapes, then society has prepared a punishment through God—he should be thrown into hell."

Hindus are also very much against the idea that Jesus can forgive you. The Christian idea is immense, tremendous, very great and full of potential. Hindus say that you will have to suffer for your past karmas; whatsoever you have done, you will have to undo. If you have done a bad thing, you will have to do something good. The bad thing and its result are going to come; you will have to suffer the consequence. Hindus will not agree with Jesus. Neither the Buddhists nor the Jainas will agree, nor were the Jews agreeing with Jesus. How can he forgive?

But I say to you—a man of that understanding can forgive. Not that by his forgiveness you are forgiven, but just that consciousness, that great consciousness can give you a feeling of well-being: "Nothing is wrong; don't be worried; you can just shake off the past like dust and get out of it." That very thing will give you such courage, such enthusiasm, will open new possibilities and new doors. You are freed from it. You immediately move beyond it. From this came the idea of the Christian confession. It does not work that way, because the man you go to confess to is an ordinary man just like you. When you are confessing, the priest is not really forgiving you; deep down, he may be condemning you. His forgiveness is just a show. He is an ordinary man; his consciousness is no higher than yours.

Only from the higher can forgiveness flow. Only from the high mountains can the rivers flow toward the plains. Only from a Jesus or a Buddha can forgiveness flow. And when there is a man like Jesus or Buddha, just his touch, just his look is enough to forgive you your whole past and all your karmas.

I totally agree with Jesus. He brings a new vision to humanity—to attain to freedom. The Hindu, Jaina, and Buddhist concept is very ordinary and mathematical. It has no magic in it. It is very logical, but it has no love in it. Jesus brings love to the world.

Enough for today.

Everyday Forgiveness:
Responses to Questions

Do you support the death penalty?

No. I don't support the death penalty for the simple reason that if somebody murders a person, and you kill that person as a penalty . . . He has committed a crime, and now the society is committing the same crime as a penalty. Through your penalty, the person who has been murdered is not going to come alive. Through your penalty, whereas there was only one person murdered, now there are two people murdered. This is sheer nonsense.

You are not being fair; you are simply taking revenge. If you were fair, you would send the murderer to a psychiatric home to be taken care of. Something is wrong in his mind; something is wrong in his psychology for which he is not responsible. He can be treated.

Not only am I against the death penalty, I am against all kinds of punishment because punishment does not change the person; in fact it makes them a harder criminal.

Every crime is basically something to do with psychology. The person's mind is not in the right shape; he needs care, he needs compassion. He needs the support of society so he can return into the society with dignity and respect.

> A civilized humanity will treat people who are criminals. They need to be sent to the hospitals, psychiatric hospitals, not to the jails.

Up to now we have been very murderous, we have been barbarous. Civilization has not happened yet. The death penalty and all kinds of punishment simply prove our barbarous approaches.

A civilized humanity will treat people who are criminals. They need to be sent to the hospitals, psychiatric hospitals, not to the jails.

What is the law of karma?

It is not in fact a law, because there is nobody behind it who is a lawgiver. On the contrary, it is intrinsic to existence itself. It is the very nature of life: whatever you sow, you reap. But it is complex: it is not so simple; it is not so obvious.

To make it clearer, try to understand it in a psychological way because the modern mind can understand only if something is explained in a psychological way. In the past, when the law of karma was talked about—when Buddha talked about it and Mahavira talked about it—they used physiological, physical analogies. We have moved far away from that. Now, people live more in the psychological, so this will be helpful.

Every crime against one's own nature—every one, without exception—records itself in our unconscious, what the Buddhists call *alaya vigyan*, the storehouse of consciousness.

Each crime—and what is a crime? It is not because of the court of Manu that it is a crime, because that court is no longer relevant; it is not because the Ten Commandments say it is a crime—that too is no longer relevant. And it is not because a certain government says it is a crime, because that goes on changing: something is a crime in Russia, and the same thing is not a crime in America. Something is a crime according to the Hindu tradition, and the same thing is not a crime according to the Mohammedan tradition. Then what is crime? There has to be a universal definition for it.

My definition is this: That which goes against your nature—that which goes against your self, your being—is a crime.

And how can you know it is a crime? Whenever you commit that crime, it is recorded in your unconsciousness. It is recorded in a certain way; it is recorded and starts giving you a feeling of guilt. You start despising yourself; you start feeling unworthy. You start feeling you are not as you should be. Something inside you becomes hard; something closes inside you. You are no longer as flowing as you were. Something has become solid, frozen. That hurts, brings pain, and brings a feeling of unworthiness.

Karen Horney has a good word to describe this unconscious

perceiving and remembering. She says, "It registers." I like it: "It registers." Everything you do registers itself automatically. If you have been loving, it registers that you are loving; it gives you a feeling of worth. If you have been hateful, angry, destructive, dishonest, it registers and gives you a feeling of unworthiness, a feeling of being something below human, a feeling of inferiority. And whenever you feel unworthy, you feel cut off from the flow of life. How can you flow with people when you are hiding something? Flow is possible only when you expose yourself, when you are available, totally available.

If you have been cheating on your woman and seeing another woman, you cannot be with your woman totally. It is impossible because it registers: deep in your unconscious you know that you have been dishonest; deep in your unconscious you know that you have betrayed; deep in your unconscious you know that you have to hide it, that you are not to reveal it. If you have something to hide, if you have something to keep secret from your beloved, there will be distance. The bigger the secret, the bigger the distance will be. If there are too many secrets, then you are completely closed. You cannot relax with this woman, and you cannot allow this woman to relax with you, because your tenseness creates tenseness in her. Her tenseness makes you even more tense, and it goes on creating a vicious circle.

Yes, it registers in our record books, in our beings. Remember, there are no record books that God is keeping. That was an old way of saying the same thing. Your being is the book. Whatever you are and whatever you do is constantly being registered. Not that there is somebody writing it; it is a natural phenomenon. If you have been lying, it is registered that you are lying, and now you have to protect those lies. And to protect one lie, you will have to tell one thousand lies, and again, to protect those one thousand lies, you will have to go on and on and on.

You become, by and by, a chronic liar. Truth becomes impossible for you because to tell one truth will be dangerous now.

See how things go together: if you tell one lie, then many lies are invited. The same attracts the same. And now truth is unwelcome because the darkness of the lies will not like the light of truth. So even when your lies are not in any danger of being exposed, you will not be able to speak the truth.

If you speak one truth, many other truths are invited. Like attracts like. If you are naturally truthful, it is very difficult to lie even once, because all that truth protects you. And this is a natural phenomenon. There is no God keeping a book. You are the book. You are the God; your being is the book.

> There is no God keeping a book. You are the book. You are the God; your being is the book.

Abraham Maslow says, "If we do something we are ashamed of, it registers to our discredit. And if we do something good, it registers to our credit." You can watch it; you can observe it.

The law of karma is not some philosophy, some abstraction. It is simply a theory which explains something true inside your being. The net result is, either we respect ourselves or we despise and feel contemptible, worthless, and unlovable.

Every moment you are creating yourself: either a grace will arise in your being or a disgrace. This is the law of karma. Nobody can avoid it. Nobody should try to cheat on karma because that is not possible. Watch, and once you understand it, things start changing. Once you know the inevitability of it, you will be a totally different person.

> Jesus said that his sacrifice on the cross was for the salvation of the world from the sins of man. Please would you comment on this?

The first thing to be understood about a man like Jesus is that whatsoever the church that is bound to grow around such a man says about him, it is bound to be wrong. What the Christian church says about Christ cannot be true. In fact, the Christian priest does not represent Christ at all. He is the same old rabbi in new garments, the same old rabbi who was responsible for Jesus's murder; the pope is not a different kind of person.

It makes no difference whether it is a Jewish establishment or a Christian establishment or a Hindu establishment; all establishments function in the same way.

Jesus is a rebel, just as Buddha is or Lao Tzu is. When the church starts establishing itself, it starts destroying the rebelliousness of Jesus or Buddha because rebellion cannot go with the establishment. It starts imposing its own ideas—once Jesus is gone, it is very easy to impose your own ideas. It starts selecting what to keep in the Bible and what not to keep. Many things have been dropped; many things have not been included in it.

For example, the Gospel of Thomas has not been included in the New Testament. It was discovered just a few years ago—and it is the most important gospel. The four gospels that have been included are nothing compared to it, but the Gospel of Thomas is very rebellious. It seems Thomas has simply reported Jesus without polluting or contaminating his message. That must have been the reason why the gospel has not been included in the authorized version of the New Testament. And those gospels that have been included, they have also been edited. For centuries, conferences went on editing them, destroying them, distorting them.

I know Jesus because I know meditation. My knowing of Jesus is not through the Bible; it is not through Christian theology. I know Jesus directly. I know Jesus because I know myself; that is my way of knowing all the buddhas.

The moment you know your own buddhahood, you have come to know all the buddhas. The experience is the same. All differences are in the mind—the moment you transcend mind, there are no differences left. How can there be differences in an absolute void? Two voids can only be exactly the same. Minds are bound to be different because they consist of thoughts. When there are clouds in the sky, then each cloud is different, but when there are no clouds at all, then the sky is one and the same.

I don't know Jesus through Christian theology; I know him directly. And my knowing is that he cannot talk in terms of sacrifice—that's the first thing, the very first. A man like Jesus does not talk in terms of sacrifice. It is celebration, not sacrifice. He is going to meet his God dancing, singing. It is not sacrifice; he is not a martyr. The Christian church tries to make him the greatest martyr, who has sacrificed himself for the salvation of the world from the sins of man. In the first place it is not sacrifice—sacrifice looks businesslike—it is celebration! Jesus is celebrating his life and his death.

Second, nobody can solve the problems of others; nobody can be the salvation of the world. And you can see it—the world is still the same. Twenty centuries have passed, and Christian priests go on talking nonsense, that Jesus sacrificed himself for the salvation of the world. But where is the salvation of the world? Either he failed, he could not manage—that they cannot accept, that he failed. Then what happened? The world seems to be exactly the same, nothing has changed. Humanity remains in the same misery.

Jesus cannot have said, "I have come for the salvation of the world." But it happens always when a church starts establishing itself: it has to create such ideas; otherwise, who is going to listen to the priests? So Jesus is salvation—not only that, but the *only* salvation.

Just the other night I was looking at a book: *Jesus, The Only Way*. Why the only way? Is Buddha not a way? Is Lao Tzu not a way? Is Zarathustra not a way? Is Moses not a way? Is Mohammed not a way? There are infinite ways to reach God. Why make

God so poor? Only one way? But the Christian priest is not interested in God, he is interested in creating a business. He has to claim that Jesus is the only way and that all other ways are wrong. He is in search of customers.

That's why every religion creates fascists and fanatics. Every religion claims, "My way is the only right way—only through me can you arrive at God. If you go on some other way, you are destined for hell, you are doomed." This is a fascist way of thinking, and it creates fanatics. All religious people are fanatics, and the world has suffered very much from this fanatical approach. It is time, the ripe time now, to drop all kinds of fascist and fanatical attitudes.

Jesus is a way, but the way has to be walked. The way can go on lying there; it is not going to help you. Just by being there, just by being crucified, Jesus cannot be the salvation of the world—otherwise, it would have happened. Then what are we doing now? Then what are the priests doing now? What is the pope doing now? If Jesus has really done the work of salvation, then there is no point in Mohammed—Mohammed came after Jesus. Then there is no point in Nanak, the founder of Sikhism, no point in Kabir coming. Jesus has closed the shop. But it has not happened.

Buddha says, "Buddhas can only point the way." But the fanatic disciples always want to make a claim. What to say about Jesus? Even Jainas claim that Mahavira came to the world for the salvation of humanity. Now it may be a little bit relevant with Jesus because he speaks in such a way that he can be very easily misinterpreted, but Mahavira is very clear. He says in absolutely definite terms that nobody can save another: "I have not come to save anybody. If I can save myself, that is enough." Even a man like Mahavira has stated this absolutely, but his disciples—the Jaina Munis and the Jaina monks and the Jaina pundits—go on claiming that Mahavira came for the salvation of humanity.

Why are people after humanity? And how can you manage it? You have not created the misery for the world, so how can you destroy it? If Jesus is the cause of the misery of the world, then certainly he can withdraw it. If he is the person who has imprisoned you, he can open the gates, unlock the doors, and tell you to leave, and you are free. But he is not the person to do it. You have done it; your hell is created by you. What can Jesus do about it?

> For our misery, for our happiness, we always want somebody else to be responsible.

But this stupid logic has gone very deep in the mind of humanity. And it is for a certain reason: we always want somebody else to be responsible. For our misery, for our happiness, we always want somebody else to be responsible.

We don't want to be responsible—to avoid responsibility, we become trapped in these kinds of ideas.

Now, Christians say Adam and Eve committed the original sin, and the whole of humanity is suffering. It is so patently foolish. Scientists say that humanity has existed for hundreds of thousands of years. Hundreds of thousands of years ago, a couple, Adam and Eve, committed a sin, and we are suffering for it—can you think of a more ridiculous thing? That you are imprisoned because all those thousands of years ago somebody committed a crime? You did not commit it; how can you suffer for it? And what original sin are they talking about? It is neither original nor sin.

What Adam did is a simple phenomenon; he disobeyed the father. Every child has to disobey the father. Unless a child disobeys the father, he never becomes mature.

It is nothing original; it is very simple and natural. It is very psychological. There comes an age when every child has to say no to the parents. If he does not say no to the parents, he will not have a spine, he will be spineless. If he cannot say no to the parents, he will be a slave his whole life. He will never attain to individuality.

Adam and Eve did not commit any sin, they simply became mature. They said no, they disobeyed. When your child goes behind the house and starts smoking, don't be worried too much; he is simply disobeying you. That is part of growth. If he never disobeys you, be worried. Take him to the psychoanalyst; something is wrong with him. If he always obeys you, then he has no soul; he is abnormal, he is not normal.

Be happy when your child disobeys you. Thank existence that now the child has started moving toward becoming an individual. It is only by disobeying, rebelling,

> It is only by disobeying, rebelling, that a child attains authentic individuality. If parents are wise, they will be happy.

that a child attains authentic individuality. If parents are wise, they will be happy.

And I think God cannot be so foolish as Christian priests. God must have been happy the day Adam and Eve disobeyed; he must have rejoiced. He must have sung a song, "Now my children are becoming mature." I can't see him being annoyed. I can't conceive of a God who cannot understand such a simple psychological phenomenon.

You have to give your God a little more intelligence than Sigmund Freud. It is such a simple fact of life that each child has to disobey. It is not sin—disobedience is not sin. And what is original about it? It is nothing unique, and it did not only happen millions of years ago; it happens each time a child starts growing. You will see it happening in your child; somewhere near the age of three or four, the child starts asserting his freedom.

That's why if you want to remember your life, you can only remember back to the age of four or at the most three; beyond that, all is dark. Why? You had no individuality, hence no memory. You attained your first individuality when you were three or four.

That's why I say this parable of Adam and Eve has so many aspects; I am never tired of talking about it from different angles. It was Eve who was the first to disobey; that means one year ahead. Adam came to his senses a little later; in fact, he was persuaded by Eve. Eve ate the fruit first, disobeyed God, and then Adam followed. This is not something that happened once, it happens always. It happens to every child, and it is good that it happens. It is at about four that the child starts feeling a kind of individuality of his own, he starts defining himself.

Lanahan, an Irish political prisoner, escaped from jail by digging a tunnel that opened into a school playground. As he emerged in the open air, Lanahan could not help shouting at a small girl, "I am free, I am free!"

"That's nothing," said the girl. "I am four."

There is a time when the child wants to declare to the world that "I am here!" that "I am!" He wants to define himself, and the only way to define himself is by disobedience. So there is nothing original about it and nothing like sin; it is a simple process of growth. And because Christianity has been denying it as a simple process of growth, it has not helped humanity to become mature.

All the religions have been trying to keep humanity immature, juvenile, childish. They are all afraid that once humanity becomes mature, then they will not be of any value, they will lose all luster. They will not be able to exploit a mature humanity; they can exploit only children.

So what sin has humanity committed so that Jesus was needed to come for the salvation of the world?

I would like to make it absolutely clear to you that there is no need for any salvation. Secondly, if you feel there is any need, it can't be done by anybody else except you, yourself. Thirdly, you are not living in sin, you are living in nature—but if nature is condemned, you start feeling guilty. And that is the trade secret of the priests: to make you feel guilty.

I don't think Jesus said that his sacrifice on the cross was for the salvation of the world from the sins of man. Priests must have imposed their ideas on Jesus. The New Testament was written centuries afterward, and then for centuries it was edited, changed, and the words that Jesus spoke were in a language that is no longer alive, Aramaic. It was not even Hebrew—a dialect of Hebrew, but different in many ways. When Jesus's words were translated, first into Greek, a great change happened; they lost their original quality, their flavor. They lost something very essential—their soul. And when from Greek and Latin they were translated into Latin and English, something was again lost. For example, you can meditate over a few words. *Repentance* is one of the key words, because Jesus uses it again and again. He says to his disciples, "Repent! Repent ye because the Day of Judgment is very close." He repeats it so many times that it must have been of tremendous value to him. But what does it mean—repent? Ask the Christian priest; he will say, "This is a simple word; everybody knows what it means: repent for your sins, repent for your guilt, repent for all that you have done." And the priest can be helpful; he can help you in the ways of repentance. But the word has nothing to do with repentance.

Jesus's word for *repent* simply means "return"; it does not mean "repentance" at all. It means, "Turn in, return to the source"; it means, "return to your own being."

That's what meditation is all about—returning to the source, returning to the center of the cyclone, returning to your very being.

Now you can see the difference. When you use the English word *repent*, it has something very ugly about it—sin, guilt, the priest, confession, this is the climate of the English word repent. But the Aramaic word simply means "return to the source," *return*. Return, don't waste time. And that's how it is with almost all key words.

It is almost impossible to understand Jesus through the priests. The only pure way, the only possible way, is to go in, to return inside. There you will meet Christ-consciousness. The only way to understand Christ is to become a christ. Never be a Christian, be a christ. Never be a Buddhist, be a buddha. Never be a Hindu, be a krishna. And if you want to be a krishna, a christ, or a buddha, then you need not go into the scriptures, and you need not ask the scholars. You will have to ask the mystics how to go in.

That's exactly what I am doing here: helping you to become aware of yourself. And the moment you know yourself, you will be surprised—you have never committed a sin.

Sin is the invention of the priest to create guilt in you. You don't need any salvation. All that you need is a little shaking up so you can wake up. You don't need priests. You certainly need awakened

> Sin is the invention of the priest to create guilt in you. You don't need any salvation. All that you need is a little shaking up so you can wake up.

people because only the awakened ones can shake those who are fast asleep and dreaming. And humanity needs to be free of guilt, free of the idea of sin, free of the idea of repentance. Humanity needs innocence, and the priests don't allow you to be innocent; they corrupt your minds.

Beware of the priests. They are the people who crucified Jesus—how can they interpret Jesus? They are the people who have always been against the buddhas, and the irony is that finally they become the interpreters.

My Jewish parents are not happy about the choices I have made for my life. What should I do?

Jesus has said, "Unless you hate your parents you cannot follow me." Now the words are very strange—and they come from a man like Jesus. They are shocking. One does not expect them, at least from Jesus because he says, "Love your enemies as you love yourself." Not only that, he even says, "Love thy neighbor as thyself"—which is far more difficult than loving your enemies! But when it comes to parents he is very clear. He says, "Unless you hate your parents you cannot follow me." Why is he so hard on parents?

But it is nothing compared to Gautam the Buddha. He used to ask his *bhikkhus*—his sannyasins, his disciples—"Have you killed your parents yet or not?" A man like Buddha, who is absolutely nonviolent! Jesus is not so nonviolent, at least he eats meat; he is not averse to eating fish. Buddha is a vegetarian, absolutely vegetarian; he is the greatest propounder of nonviolence on the earth. And he asks his disciples again and again, "Have you killed your parents yet or not?"

Of course they don't mean it literally, neither Jesus nor Buddha, but their words are significant. What they really mean is a great message; it is metaphoric. You will have to understand the metaphor. They are not concerned with the outer parents, your father and mother; they are concerned with the inner imprints that your mother and father have created in you.

It is not the outer parents who are dominating you. What can they do? You are here, and they may be thousands of miles away somewhere in Germany. What can they do? They cannot dominate you. But you have something inner: you have inner ideas, inner reflections, imprints, impressions of your parents, and those ideas go on dominating you. If they don't like the choices you have made for your life, then your conscience will feel guilt. You will feel that you are hurting your parents; that it is not good, that this should not be so, that something has to be done. But parents are always against anything that is new.

Buddha's father was not happy with him; he was very unhappy, he was angry at him. Buddha had to escape out of his kingdom—he was afraid that he would be caught because detectives were sent to catch hold of him. He was the only son of his father, and the father was getting old; the father was seventy when Buddha escaped from his home. The father was afraid—who was going to possess his kingdom? And stories were coming to him, rumors, gossip of all kinds: that Buddha had become a monk, that he was begging, that he had become a beggar. And, of course, the old king was getting very angry: "What is this nonsense? The son of a king begging—for what? He has everything—why should he beg? And he is begging from house to house, walking barefoot and surrounded by other beggars like himself. What is he doing? He has betrayed me in my old age!"

Naturally he was angry, but the real anger is somewhere else. The anger is because Buddha has gone against his religion, his ideology. He has gone against all that the father represents—he has gone against the ego of the father.

Jesus's parents were not happy with Jesus either. They were orthodox Jews; how could they be happy with a son who was preaching strange things and who was talking in such a way as if he knew more than Moses? Because Jesus was saying again and again, "It was said to you in the past, but I say unto you that it is wrong. It was told to you that if somebody throws a brick at you, answer him by throwing a rock at him. But I say to you, if somebody hits one of your cheeks, give him the other cheek too."

Now this was absolutely against the Jewish idea of justice; this seemed almost anti-Jewish because even the Jewish God declares in the Talmud, "I am a very jealous God. If you go against me, I will destroy you."

And he destroyed two cities completely. What happened in Hiroshima and Nagasaki, the Jewish God had done three thousand years before! He destroyed two cities for the simple reason that people were not behaving according to his idea of morality, they were becoming immoral. He destroyed two whole cities.

Now, all the people could not have been immoral, and even if all the people had been immoral, they could not have been immoral to the same degree. There were small children also; they could not have been immoral. They didn't know anything of morality or immorality. There were very old people also; they could not have been immoral. There were ill people, who could not even get out of their beds—what immoral acts could they have been doing? But he was so angry that he destroyed two whole cities just to teach a lesson to humanity.

And this young man Jesus is saying, "Forgive." He was going against all the ideas of the Judaic religion completely. He was teaching people new concepts, new visions, new ways of approaching God. The parents were angry.

Once it happened that Jesus was teaching, surrounded by his disciples and a crowd also. His mother came, and somebody informed him from the crowd, "Your mother is waiting outside, and she wants to see you urgently." Jesus is reported to have said, "Tell that woman"—not "my mother"—he says, "Tell that woman that nobody is my father and nobody is my mother and nobody is my relative. All my relatives are those who are with me. I have nothing to do with those who are not with me. Tell her to go away."

It seems hard, it seems cruel, but there is a reason in it. These are all symbolic stories; I don't think it really happened. I don't think Jesus would say, "Tell that woman . . ." But it says something. You have to drop the idea of your father, of your mother, from your innermost core; only then do you become mature. If you carry that idea, you remain childish; you never become mature. And no father, no mother ever wants you to become really mature because maturity will mean that you will become free.

All the so-called religions have taught you to respect your parents for the simple reason that if you respect your parents, you will respect the past. You will respect traditions; you will respect conventions. If you respect your father, you will respect God the Father. If you don't respect your parents, then naturally you are cut off from tradition and no church can afford it.

I will not say to you don't respect your father and mother. I will say to you that you can respect your father and mother only when you are completely free of your inner impressions of father and mother; otherwise, your respect is false, pseudo. You can love your father and mother only when you are completely free of them; otherwise, you cannot love them. You will remain angry with them. Nobody can love anybody unless one becomes free of that person. If there is dependence of any kind, love remains only a facade; deep down there is hatred. And every child hates his father and mother—every child, without exception. But respect is imposed from the outside.

Just look within your unconscious; look deep down within yourself, and you will find a great revengeful fire. You want to take revenge on your parents. You are angry because they are responsible for the way you are. It is the way they have brought you up that is making you miserable. It is the way they have conditioned you that is making you crippled and paralyzed. Hence, naturally, there is hatred.

I would like you to become aware of it so that you can drop it, because whatsoever they have done, they have done unconsciously. They need to be forgiven. Forgive them.

Jesus says, "Hate your father and mother." Buddha says, "Kill them." I say to you to forgive them—which is far more difficult. Forgive them, because whatsoever they have done, they have done unknowingly; they were conditioned by their parents, and so on and so forth.

> Jesus says, "Hate your father and mother." Buddha says, "Kill them." I say to you to forgive them—which is far more difficult.

Even Adam and Eve were conditioned by their father, God. Conditioning begins there. God is responsible for conditioning Adam: "Don't eat the fruit from the Tree of Knowledge." That "don't" became an attraction; that is a negative way of conditioning. And if it is said emphatically that you shouldn't do a certain thing, a great urge arises in you to experiment, to experience it. Why? Why is God so interested? Because the Tree of Knowledge cannot be a bad thing; knowing cannot be bad. If you become wise, what is wrong? Wisdom is good; knowledge is good.

Certainly Adam must have thought to himself, "God is trying to keep me from becoming as wise as he is, so that I always remain dependent on him, so that I always have go to him for his advice, so that I can never live on my own, so that I always have to be just a shadow to him. He does not want me to be free and independent." That is a simple, logical conclusion.

And that's also what the Devil did—he argued the same thing. He told Eve . . . why had he chosen Eve, not Adam? Because if you persuade the wife, if the wife is convinced, then you need not worry about the husband. Every advertising expert knows this; hence most advertisements are meant for women. Once they are convinced, then nobody can unconvince them, at least not their husbands: they have to follow suit; they have to do it because the woman will become a continuous torture if you don't do it.

The Devil was the first advertising expert. He was the pioneer, he was the founder of the whole art. He did not bother about Adam—he must have known that all husbands are henpecked, so why bother about them? Persuade the wife. He persuaded her, and of course she was convinced because the logic was so clear. He said, "God has prohibited it only because he does not want you to become like gods. Once you eat the fruit of the Tree of Knowledge, you will be like gods. And he is jealous, he is afraid. It will be foolish on your part if you don't eat. Be like gods!"

And who would not like to be like a god? Once the temptation was there, it was impossible to resist. But all of the conditioning came from God himself; it was a negative kind of conditioning.

Your parents are not responsible, really. An unconscious person cannot be held responsible; he functions unconsciously, he does not know what he is doing.

You have to go within yourself and cleanse yourself of all the impressions that your parents have put upon you, both negative and positive. Then there will arise great compassion in you for your parents, great compassion and great gratitude also, because whatsoever they have done, they have done—according to them, at least—thinking that it is good. They have not deliberately done anything wrong to you. Even now, if they are against your choices, if they are not happy with your choices, it is because they think you have fallen into wrong hands, that you have fallen from their traditional heritage. They are afraid you may go astray, you may suffer later on, you may repent one day. They feel for you.

Their love is unconscious, hence you need not listen to them, but you are not to become angry with them; you have to understand them.

You say: "My Jewish parents are not happy with the choices I have made for my life." First, they are Jewish. That is one of the oldest religions in the world. There are only two old religions in the world: the Judaic religion and the Hindu religion. The older a tradition, the greater is its weight; it crushes people more. Anything new is light.

My people can walk light-footedly, almost dancingly. But a five-thousand-year-old tradition creates a great weight; it is a long past. They could not forgive Jesus; how can they forgive you? And Jesus has not become one of my people! In fact, he never went outside the tradition; he remained a Jew. He was not a Christian, remember, because there was no Christianity at that time. Christianity was born out of his death, out of his crucifixion. Hence I always call Christianity "Crossianity"; it has nothing to do with Christ, it has something to do with the cross. That's why the cross has become the symbol of Christianity—far more important than Christ.

They could not forgive Jesus, and he never went outside the tradition. Of course he was saying things that looked a little strange, a little new. He was bringing new light; he was clearing the mirror of the Jewish consciousness from the old dust.

To become one of my people is certainly far more dangerous because it is going totally out of all traditions. It is not just changing one tradition for another, it is dropping the very traditional mind itself. It is dropping being traditional as such; it is becoming nontraditional, unconventional. It is pure revolution! And they are afraid, naturally. For many reasons, they are afraid.

And there is some attraction between me and the Jews. I have attracted so many Jews here that sometimes I myself wonder—am I a Jew, or what is the matter?—because Jews are not so easily attracted to anybody. They were not attracted to Jesus. They are not attracted to anybody else. Why have they come to me? I have touched something deep in them. In fact, they have suffered from tradition more than anybody else; that's the reason why they have become so interested in my vision—because I am anti-traditional. They would like to get rid of it.

A Jew and a Black man are sitting next to each other on the train. Suddenly the Jew realizes that the Black man is reading a Hebrew magazine. He keeps silent for a while, then whispers to him: "Listen, friend, is it not enough to be a Black?"

Your parents may be afraid: "Is it not enough to be a Jew? Now you want to suffer more?" Because to be with me is going to be dangerous. Freedom is far more dangerous than anything else in the world. Freedom is fire: it burns your ego, and because it makes you egoless it hurts many other people's egos and they all become enemies to you.

And then Jews are very worldly people. It is the only religion that is very worldly. There are two kinds of religions: the worldly religions—Jews represent the worldly religion—and there are the otherworldly religions, for example, Buddhism. Buddhists will be against me because to them I will look a little worldly, and to Jews I will look a little too otherworldly.

I am both: I am a bridge. My vision is a synthesis because I don't divide "this world" and "that world." To me they are both beautiful. And one has to live in both worlds together because they are not separate. They are inseparable. The very idea of dividing them was a great calamity.

Jews are more interested in the worldly than in the otherworldly. Now, thinking that you have become a meditator, they will be afraid: "What are you doing? This is the time to earn money. This is the time to get rooted in the world. Don't waste this precious time!" According to them, when you are young you can do something; as you become old you will be less and less able to make money, to have power, prestige, to make a name in the world. You are wasting your time.

Your parents must be worried about what you are doing here. Such an intelligent guy like you, wasting his time meditating? Have you gone crazy or something, sitting silently doing nothing? Is this a way a Jew is supposed to behave? Time is money—

don't waste it! And, moreover, whether your parents are Jewish or not, parents are parents. They feel offended—they feel offended by the very idea that you think you know more than they know, that you are trying new ways, that you are trying to be wiser than your parents.

A Jew arrives in heaven and God, in a very compassionate voice, asks, "What happened to you?"

He says, "I was brokenhearted. When my only son, my pride and my joy, announced that he had become Catholic, I felt this terrible pain in my chest . . ."

"You should not have despaired so much. Even my only son did the same!"

"And what did you do, my Lord?"

"I made a new will and testament!"

So, what can they do? They will make a new will and a new testament—let them make it! Learn to forgive them. I will not tell you to hate them, because hate is not freedom. If you hate somebody, you remain attached.

Hate is a relationship. Love is freedom. Love is not a relationship; hate is a relationship.

That's why those who live in relationship live in hate, not in love. Love is freedom. Love them, then you are free. But to love them, you will have to cleanse yourself totally.

I will not tell you, like Gautam the Buddha, to kill them, because killing is not going to help. Understand them. Be compassionate. Killing will be doing something in a hurry; there is no need to be in a hurry. And parents have gone so deep in you. They are not only in your blood and bones; they have entered your very marrow. You cannot kill them easily—it is impossible. You will have to commit suicide if you want to kill them, because only then will they be killed. They have entered your being: you are part of them, they are part of you. But through deep understanding you can be free of them.

I will not suggest killing your mother; my methods are far more subtle. What Jesus said and what Buddha said are very primitive methods. What I am saying is far more sophisticated— forgive your parents, understand them. The whole question is within you; it has nothing to do with the outer parents. If you can relax within yourself, and if you can feel compassion for them, because they have suffered in their own way . . . They have wasted their whole life, now they want to waste your life because that is the only way they know how to live. Great compassion is bound to arise in you, and out of that compassion maybe you can be of some help to them, because compassion functions in a very subtle way. Love is the greatest magic in the world.

I will not tell you to go and listen to them and follow them to satisfy them; that will be wrong. That will be destroying your life, and it will not help them either. You have to remain yourself and yet be compassionate and forgiving. And if you happen to go there, remain compassionate and forgiving. Let them feel your compassion, your love, your joy. Let them feel your celebration.

Let them feel what has happened to you through being here. Let them see the difference.

Buddha's father remained angry until Buddha came to see him. He was so full of anger when he saw him that for a few moments he could even not see. Buddha remained silent. The father went on insulting him, saying, "You have been a deep wound to me—you have almost killed me! Why have you come now after twelve years? I have waited so long. You have not been a son to me, you have been an enemy!"

Buddha listened and did not utter a single word. Then the father suddenly became aware that the son had not even spoken a single word. He asked, "Why are you not speaking?"

Buddha said, "First say everything that you have carried for all these twelve years. Cathart, unburden yourself! Only when you are unburdened will you be able to see me. There is one thing that I would like to say to you: that you are now talking to somebody else, not to your son. The man who had left your palace has not come back—he has died. I am a totally new man. I have come with new consciousness, with new love, with new compassion. But first unburden yourself; otherwise, your eyes are so full of rage you cannot see me. Let your eyes be cleared."

The father was trembling with anger. Slowly he cooled down; this very answer cooled him. Tears of anger were coming to his eyes. He wiped his tears, looked again. "Yes, this is not the same man who left my palace; this is a totally different person. Of course, the face is the same, the figure is the same, but it is a totally new being—the vibe is new."

He fell at the feet of Buddha, and he said, "Initiate me too, because now I am very old; death is coming closer. I would also like to taste something that you have tasted. And forgive me and forgive all my anger. I have not known what is happening to you and what has happened to you. It is good that you have come. It is good that you remembered me, that you have not forgotten me."

So whenever you go back, let them first cathart. And remember, they are German parents, so they will cathart longer than Buddha's parent! Listen silently. Don't get angry. If you really want to help them, remain meditative, calm, and quiet, and your coolness will transform them.

And each person should want to help his parents because they have given birth to you. They have brought you up in the only way they could; it was not possible for them to do otherwise. Whatsoever they could do, they have done, and they have done it for your good. Whether it proved good or not is another matter, but their intentions were good. So whenever you go back, remember to help them.

Postscript

Looking at others is just a way of avoiding looking at oneself. Whenever you criticize somebody else, watch: it is a trick of the mind so that you can forgive yourself. People go on criticizing others; when they criticize the whole world they feel very good. In comparison, they can think they are not worse than other people; in fact, they are better. That's why when you criticize somebody you exaggerate, you go to the very extreme, you make a mountain out of a molehill. You go on making the mountain bigger and bigger and bigger, then your own mountain looks very small. You feel happy.

Stop this. This is not going to help you.

All About OSHO

Your Most Important Web Link
OSHO.com/AllAboutOSHO

This website is a comprehensive online portal to all things OSHO, including information about his books and meditation techniques, audio and video recordings of his talks, and searchable text archives of his talks in English and in Hindi. Here you can find apps for your phone or subscribe to a "no-thought for the day," pick a card or do a reading with the OSHO Zen Tarot. You can find out how to subscribe to a regular newsletter or sign up as a subscriber to OSHO Radio and OSHO TV. There's a shop where you can find music for the OSHO Active Meditations or meditative music just for listening.

This page is regularly updated to let you know about new book releases and what's new in the OSHO TIMES online newspaper. It is regularly refreshed with features and excerpts from Osho's talks that address the most common questions people have about Osho and his work or shed light on the most pressing social, political, and environmental issues of our time.

An entire section of this page is devoted to the OSHO Meditations, with frequent updates and helpful content for those experimenting with these methods. Another section covers the programs and facilities offered at the OSHO International Meditation Resort in Pune, India, where an in-depth experience of Osho's vision of a meditative lifestyle can be experienced.

OSHO International Online also offers an expanding program of online meditations, courses, groups, OSHO Meditative Therapies, individual sessions, and other learning opportunities—all developed to dive deeper into and to discover your own being.

To contact **OSHO INTERNATIONAL ONLINE:**
www.osho.com/oshointernational, oshointernational@osho-international.com

About the Author

Osho defies categorization. His thousands of talks cover everything from the individual quest for meaning to the most urgent social and political issues facing society today. Osho's books are not written, but are transcribed from audio and video recordings of his extemporaneous talks to international audiences. As he puts it, "So remember: whatever I am saying is not just for you . . . I am talking also for the future generations."

Osho has been described by the *Sunday Times* in London as one of the "1000 Makers of the 20th Century" and by American author Tom Robbins as "the most dangerous man since Jesus Christ." *Sunday Mid-Day* (India) has selected Osho as one of ten people—along with Gandhi, Nehru, and Buddha—who have changed the destiny of India. About his own work Osho has said that he is helping to create the conditions for the birth of a new kind of human being. He often characterizes this new human being as "Zorba the Buddha"—capable both of enjoying the earthy pleasures of a Zorba the Greek and the silent serenity of a Gautama the Buddha. Running like a thread through all aspects of

Osho's talks and meditations is a vision that encompasses both the timeless wisdom of all ages past and the highest potential of today's (and tomorrow's) science and technology.

Osho is known for his revolutionary contribution to the science of inner transformation, with an approach to meditation that acknowledges the accelerated pace of contemporary life. His unique OSHO Active Meditations are designed to first release the accumulated stresses of body and mind, so that it is then easier to take an experience of stillness and thought-free relaxation into daily life.

Two autobiographical works by the author are *Autobiography of a Spiritually Incorrect Mystic* (St. Martin's Press) and *Glimpses of a Golden Childhood*.